365 Drawing Prompts

2020 Edition

Written by Jaz Johnson

Edited by Jaz Johnson & Brandon Tate

Formatted by Jaz Johnson

Cover Design by Jaz Johnson

First paperback edition published January 1st, 2020.

ISBN: 978-1-951626-08-2 (e-book)

ISBN: 978-1-951626-09-9 (paperback)

Published by TC Studios LLC

www.TCStudiosHQ.com

Table Of Contents

Introductions

Hello! Welcome to our 2020 edition of *365 Drawing Prompts*. This book is a party of our creative group, **Prompt Party**. It's going to get your creative mojo flowing and make you want to start drawing!

This book includes the following:

1. 365 drawing prompts in eight different mediums (a) and twelve different themes (b).
    a. Pencil (P), Color Pencil (CP), Acrylic Paint (AP), Marker (M), Crayon (C), Gouache (G), Watercolor (W,) Ink (I).
    b. People & Places, Texture, Poses, Animals, Plants, Technology, Emotion, Magic, Clothes, Self-Care, Colors, Food & Beverages.
2. 73 drawing exercises.

How To Use Our Prompts

Each prompt will list a hypothetical situation and a few suggested mediums to draw with, as well as suggested paths you can take with the prompt. You are **not** required to draw in with mediums or to use the brainstorming sections. They are **only suggestions**.

Some prompts talk about you, but you don't always have to draw yourself. You can make up a character, or characters to draw, too!

The goal is to draw or paint a picture using the prompts provided.

Share Your Work & Tag Us

We would love to be able to see the amazing things you come up with and tell you how much we love them.

To do that, all you have to do is post your work to Facebook, Instagram or Twitter and tag us @PromptParty. Then we'll be able to see and comment on them!

Submit To Our Anthologies

Would you like your work to be published? Kids and teens just like you are using our prompt books across the country, and many of them are submitting their work to our annual anthologies.

An anthology is a collection of work by many different people. Each year, we publish one with work that is made using our drawing prompts.

Ten percent of each of our anthologies goes back into helping communities like yours. This money goes towards public school donations, public library donations, and more. So, help your community out by getting more people involved!

For more details on our mission to give back to communities across the country, visit our website, www.TCStudiosHQ.com.

To submit your work to our anthology, please do the following:

- Send an email to submissions@tcstudioshq.com with the following:
  - **Subject Line:**
    - 365 Drawing Prompts Anthology Submission (2020)
  - **Body:**
    - First and last name (or pen/artist name).
    - The medium you used.
  - **Attachments:**
    - Attached work.
      - Attached as a **PNG** for art.
      - Attached signed publication form.
        - You can find this on our website.

If you are selected, we will reach out to you to request more information.

For more information on our other anthologies and an in-depth guide on how to submit to them, visit our website, www.TCStuidiosHQ.com.

Check Out Our Work

Did you know that we also publish novels, comics, and other creative guides?

To find out more about everything we publish and where you can read/get them, visit our website, www.TCStudiosHQ.com.

Chapter One: People & Places.

\#1 – Ballerina. (CP) (W) (M)

Brainstorm …

- Are they dancing?
    - Are they performing?
    - What kind of outfit are they wearing?
    - Do they have a partner?
- Are they practicing?
    - How old are they?
    - Are they skilled, or a beginner?

Brainstorm …

- Challenge: Monochrome.
    - Try drawing this scene using only one gradient of color.

You can share your work with us on Facebook, Instagram & Twitter!

Tag us @PromptParty and use #PromptParty.

We'd love to see what you come up with!

#2 – Police Station. (G) (I) (AP)

Brainstorm …

- Are there any criminals there?
  - Has someone been arrested? What for?
- Where are the police?
  - Are they slacking off?
  - Are they working on a case?

Brainstorm …

- Experiment: Colored Lighting.
  - When/if you are applying lighting effects to this piece, try using a different color instead of just a lighter gradient of the lit area.

Do you want your work published?

You can submit any work made using our prompts to our annual anthologies! Published submissions receive shared 25% royalties.

You can find more information on our website, www.TCStudiosHQ.com.

#3 – Mountain. (P) (C) (M)

Brainstorm …

- What's the weather like?
  - Is there snow? Lush fields?
  - Is it storming, or a beautiful day?
- Are people climbing it?
  - Are they excited? Scared? Tired?
  - Are there any animals on it?

Brainstorm …

- Focus on: Background.
  - Tell the story with the use of the background and its environment. Think about the use and placement of specific items to help get the point across.

Did you know?

A percentage of every anthology sold goes towards helping communities like yours. This includes donations to charities, funding of scholarships, creating of programs, and more!

You can find more information on our website, www.TCStudiosHQ.com.

#4 – Doctor. (AP) (W) (G)

Brainstorm …

- What kind of doctor are they?
    - Are they with a patient?
    - Do they have a nurse?
- What tools might they use?

Brainstorm …

- Practice: Hair.
    - Study the flow and lighting dimensions of hair and implement the techniques into your drawing.

Did you know?

In addition to our annual prompt anthologies, every year we have <u>themed</u> anthologies that you can also submit to!

You can find more information on our website, www.TCStudiosHQ.com.

#5 – Meadow. (I) (CP) (C)

Brainstorm …

- What kinds of flowers are there?
- Are there animals around? People?
- Is there any running water?

Brainstorm …

- Challenge: No Linework.
    - Try drawing this scene with no outlining – just dive right in with blocks of color!

Drawing Exercise #1

Go out and sketch your favorite place to hang out.

\#6 – Mentor. (W) (AP) (G)

Brainstorm …

- What are they teaching? Who are they teaching?
  - What things might they need to help them teach?
  - Who are the students?

Brainstorm …

- Experiment: Comic Strip.
  - Try drawing this as a short comic strip.

Looking for a challenge?

Try doing one of our prompts with your friend(s)! See if you can
come up with something together.

#7 – Tiny House. (P) (W) (I)

Brainstorm ...

- What would your perfect tiny house look like?
- What if you drew the interior?
- What if you drew the building process?
- Is it parked with other tiny houses?
- Who lives in it?

Brainstorm ...

- Challenge: Color Palette.
    - Use a random color palette generator or ask a friend to pick 3-5 colors for you to use.

Did you know?

We also make books to help with storytelling. With help on things like creating characters, world-building, magic systems, and more!

You can find more information on our website,
www.TCStudiosHQ.com.

\#8 – Parents. (M) (C) (AP)

Brainstorm …

- How many kids do they have? How old are they?
- Are they pet parents? To what animals?
- What's a positive memory you have with your parent(s)?
- What's a negative memory you have with your parent(s)?
- Are you a parent?
  - What's a day in your life look like?

Brainstorm …

- Life Study.
  - Go out and find a person with this prompt to sketch.
  - See if someone you know will let you draw them!

Did you know?

We also publish novels and comics that you can read!

You can find more information on our website,
www.TCStudiosHQ.com.

#9 – Fort. (G) (I) (C)

Brainstorm …

- Pillow fort? Tree fort?
- Is it hidden? Is it secret? Does it have a password?
- Has it been built yet?
  - Maybe they're putting together a blueprint.
- What's inside the fort?
- Who's inside the fort?

Brainstorm …

- Practice different types of shading techniques.
  - Hatching.
  - Cross-Hatching.
  - Stippling.
  - Scribbling.
  - Contour Lines.

Do you want to give us a prompt for next year's edition?

You can submit prompt ideas you have based on next year's chapter themes. Credit will be given if selected.

You can find more information on our website, www.TCStudiosHQ.com.

#10 – Child. (W) (AP) (P)

Brainstorm …

- What are they doing?
- Are they in trouble?
- Are they playing?

Brainstorm …

- Practice: Skin Tones.
    - Study skin tone palettes and techniques and implement them in your drawing.

Drawing Exercise #2

Draw a realistic portrait of your best friend.

#11 – Beach. (G) (M) (CP)

Brainstorm ...

- What time of day is it?
- How many people are there?
- Is there a date happening?
- Are there activities happening in the water?
- Are there animals around?

Brainstorm ...

- Practice: Lighting.
  - Study color choice, gradients, and placement techniques of lighting and implement them in your drawing.

Did you know?

We post daily writing & drawing prompts on our Social Medias for everyone to participate in.

Find us @PromptParty and use #PromptParty.

You can find more information on our website, www.TCStudiosHQ.com.

\#12 – Hero/Heroine. (I) (P) (W)

Brainstorm …

- What does their outfit look like?
- Do they have any powers?
- Do they have a sidekick?
- Do they have a hideout/base?

Brainstorm …

- Focus on: Body Language.
  - How can you position the body to emphasize this prompt?

Did you know?

In addition to posting daily on Social Media, we have daily interactive posts on our YouTube channel, Podcast, and Blog.

You can find more information on our website, www.TCStudiosHQ.com.

#13 – Witch. (AP) (M) (I)

Brainstorm …

- Evil witch? Good witch?
- Spice up their outfit.
- What items do they have/need?

Brainstorm …

- Experiment: Colored Lighting.
  - When/if you are applying lighting effects to this piece, try using a different color instead of just a lighter gradient of the lit area.

Remember!

The listed genres/mediums and brainstorming boxes are **only suggestions!** We encourage you to do/use whatever you want.

#14 – Temple. (C) (G) (CP)

Brainstorm …

- Where is it located? Jungle? Desert? Ocean?
- Is it in good condition?
- What is the décor like?
- Are there traps?
- Is someone exploring it? Why?
  - What are they looking for?

Brainstorm …

- Challenge: Secondary Colors.
  - Try drawing this scene using only secondary colors and their gradients.

You can share your work with us on Facebook, Instagram & Twitter!

Tag us @PromptParty and use #PromptParty.

We'd love to see what you come up with!

#15 – City. (M) (G) (I)

Brainstorm …

- Is it big? Small?
- What's happening?
  - o   Maybe a festival? A disaster? A crime? A protest?
- What do you like to do in the city?

Brainstorm (Drawing) …

- Challenge: Opposite Colors.
  - o   Pick a color and its opposite (ex: red and green).
  - o   Try coloring this piece with only those two colors and their gradients.

Drawing Exercise #3

Draw the exterior of your dream home.

#16 – Concert. (W) (AP) (C)

Brainstorm …

- What kind of band/artist is performing?
  - Is the crowd having a good time?
- Is it inside? Outside?
  - What's the weather like?
  - What is the interior of the building like?

Brainstorm …

- Experiment: Bold Line Work.
  - When you've finished lining your work (if you're lining), try making some areas thicker than others.
    - It can be dramatically, or just a bit.
      - Take note of how it changes the tone of your work.

Do you want your work published?

You can submit any work made using our prompts to our annual anthologies! Published submissions receive shared 25% royalties.

You can find more information on our website,
www.TCStudiosHQ.com.

\#17 – Band. (P) (M) (CP)

Brainstorm …

- What kind of band is it?
- How many members are there?
    - How old are they?
    - What do they play/do?
- Do they all get along?

Brainstorm …

- Practice: Hands.
    - Study up on some hand techniques and implement them in your drawing.
        - Maybe they're holding a microphone or an instrument.

Did you know?

A percentage of every anthology sold goes towards helping communities like yours. This includes donations to charities, funding of scholarships, creating of programs, and more!

You can find more information on our website, www.TCStudiosHQ.com.

#18 – Spy/Secret Agent. (AP) (G) (I)

Brainstorm …

- Are they on a mission?
    - Is it dangerous? Boring?
- Have they been discovered?
- Do they have a spouse?
    - Does the spouse know they're a spy?

Brainstorm …

- Experiment: Comic Strip.
    - Try drawing this as a short comic strip.

Did you know?

In addition to our annual prompt anthologies, every year we have
<u>themed</u> anthologies that you can also submit to!

You can find more information on our website,
www.TCStudiosHQ.com.

\#19 – Model. (M) (W) (P)

Brainstorm …

- What are they modeling?
- Are they in a photo shoot?
- Are they walking on a runway?
- Is their outfit crazy? Elegant? Trendy?
- Are they young? Old? Plus-sized?

Brainstorm …

- Focus on: Body Language.
    - How can you position the body to emphasize this prompt?

Looking for a challenge?

Try doing one of our prompts with your friend(s)! See if you can come up with something together.

\#20 – Space. (I) (C) (CP)

Brainstorm …

- Are there astronauts exploring?
- Are there aliens roaming?
- What constellations can you see?

Brainstorm …

- Challenge: No Linework.
    - Try drawing this scene with no outlining – just dive right in with blocks of color!

Drawing Exercise #4

Draw what your house looks like during your favorite holiday.

#21 – Tropical Island. (G) (M) (CP)

Brainstorm …

- Are there people? A civilization?
  - o   Are they stranded?
  - o   Are they trying to leave?
- What kind of animals are there?
- How did they get there?
- What is the weather like?
- What kind of plant life is there?

Brainstorm …

- Challenge: Bird's Eye View.
  - o   Try drawing this piece with a bird's eye view.

Did you know?

We also make books to help with storytelling. With help on things like creating characters, world-building, magic systems, and more!

You can find more information on our website,
www.TCStudiosHQ.com.

#22 – Scientist. (AP) (I) (W)

Brainstorm …

- What are they working on?
- Are they an evil scientist?
- Do they have work partners?
- What does their workspace look like?

Brainstorm …

- Practice: Hands.
  - Study up on some hand techniques and implement them in your drawing.
    - Maybe they're mixing chemicals or cleaning their goggles.

Did you know?

We also publish novels and comics that you can read!

You can find more information on our website,
www.TCStudiosHQ.com.

#23 – House. (W) (CP) (I)

Brainstorm ...

- What does the exterior design look like?
- What does the interior design look like?
- Is there a front yard? Is there a back yard?
- Is there a garden? A garage? A car?

Brainstorm ...

- Focus on: Background.
    - Tell the story with the use of the background and its environment. Think about the use and placement of specific items to help get the point across.

Do you want to give us a prompt for next year's edition?

You can submit prompt ideas you have based on next year's chapter themes. Credit will be given if selected.

You can find more information on our website, www.TCStudiosHQ.com.

#24 – Inventor. (M) (G) (C)

Brainstorm …

- What are they inventing?
- Have they invented other things?
  - What do they do?
- Do they have an assistant?

Brainstorm …

- Experiment: Exaggerated Proportions/Features.
  - Get a little cartoony.
  - How might exaggerating certain features help the imagery?

Did you know?

We post daily writing & drawing prompts on our Social Medias for everyone to participate in.

Find us @PromptParty and use #PromptParty.

You can find more information on our website, www.TCStudiosHQ.com.

\#25 – Circus. (P) (I) (W)

Brainstorm ...

- Who is performing?
- Are there any weird acts?
- Is there a large crowd? Are they excited?

Brainstorm ...

- Challenge: Color Palette.
    - Use a random color palette generator or ask a friend to pick 3-5 colors for you to use.

Drawing Exercise #5

Draw yourself as a fantasy creature (i.e. elf, orc, etc.)

#26 – Artist. (M) (CP) (G)

<table>
<tr><td>

Brainstorm …

- What kind of artist are they?
    - Performing? Visual? Musical?
- Are they working on a project?
- How do they interact with their fan base?
- Do they have a style/aesthetic?

</td></tr>
</table>

<table>
<tr><td>

Brainstorm …

- Life Study.
    - Go out and find a person with this prompt to sketch.
    - See if someone you know will let you draw them!

</td></tr>
</table>

Did you know?

In addition to posting daily on Social Media, we have daily interactive posts on our YouTube channel, Podcast, and Blog.

You can find more information on our website,
www.TCStudiosHQ.com.

#27 – Athlete. (P) (AP) (CP)

Brainstorm …

- What sport do they play?
- Do they have a workout routine?
- Do they have a special diet?
- Do they have a team?
  - Do they hang out?

Brainstorm …

- Challenge: No references.
  - Put your muscle memory to the test and draw this scene without using any references.
    - Good luck!

Remember!

The listed genres/mediums and brainstorming boxes are **only suggestions!** We encourage you to do/use whatever you want.

#28 – Alien. (I) (M) (W)

Brainstorm …

- Are they friendly? Dangerous?
- What are they doing?
    - Abducting someone? Trying to communicate?
- Where did they come from?
- Have they been captured?

Brainstorm …

- Practice: Skin Tones.
    - Study skin tone palettes and techniques and implement them in your drawing.

You can share your work with us on Facebook, Instagram & Twitter!

Tag us @PromptParty and use #PromptParty.

We'd love to see what you come up with!

#29 – Amusement Park. (G) (I) (C)

> **Brainstorm ...**
>
> - What kind of rides are there?
> - Are a group of friends there? Is there a date?
> - What kind of food is there?
> - Try exploring this prompt in photos.

> **Brainstorm ...**
>
> - Challenge: Input.
>   - Let someone tell you how you should set up your drawing and follow their instructions to the best of your ability.

Do you want your work published?

You can submit any work made using our prompts to our annual anthologies! Published submissions receive shared 25% royalties.

You can find more information on our website,
www.TCStudiosHQ.com.

#30 – Dungeon. (P) (AP) (W)

Brainstorm …

- What kind of dungeon is it?
  - Torture? Monster?
- What's in it? Who's in it?
- Is it hidden? Where is it located?

Brainstorm …

- Experiment: Bold Line Work.
  - When you've finished lining your work (if you're lining), try making some areas thicker than others.
    - It can be dramatically, or just a bit.
      - Take note of how it changes the tone of your work.

Drawing Exercise #6

Draw yourself in your ideal career.

\#31 – Bookstore. (G) (CP) (W)

Brainstorm …

- Is it a used book store?
- Is it big? Small?
- What kind of books do they have?
- Is there a café?
- What are some books on your To-Be-Read list?

Brainstorm …

- Practice: Lighting.
  - Study color choice, gradients, and placement techniques of lighting and implement them in your drawing.

Did you know?

A percentage of every anthology sold goes towards helping communities like yours. This includes donations to charities, funding of scholarships, creating of programs, and more!

You can find more information on our website, www.TCStudiosHQ.com.

Chapter Two: Texture.

#32 – Slimy. (M) (CP) (G)

<table>
<tr><td>

Brainstorm …

- What's something that's slimy?
- Slime monster?
- Is it toxic? Radioactive?

</td></tr>
</table>

<table>
<tr><td>

Brainstorm …

- Challenge: No Linework.
  - Try drawing this scene with no outlining – just dive right in with blocks of color!

</td></tr>
</table>

Did you know?

In addition to our annual prompt anthologies, every year we have <u>themed</u> anthologies that you can also submit to!

You can find more information on our website,
www.TCStudiosHQ.com.

#33 – Dry. (P) (AP) (I)

Brainstorm ...

- Skin? The desert? Hot weather?
- What might that texture look like?
- Try a combination of dry things.

Brainstorm ...

- Practice different types of shading techniques.
    - Hatching.
    - Cross-Hatching.
    - Stippling.
    - Scribbling.
    - Contour Lines.

Did you know?

In addition to our annual prompt anthologies, every year we have themed anthologies that you can also submit to!

You can find more information on our website,
www.TCStudiosHQ.com.

#34 – Wrinkled. (M) (W) (CP)

Brainstorm …

- Skin? Clothing?
- Someone in wrinkly, comfortable clothing.
- An elderly person.
- Pruned fingers.

Brainstorm …

- Challenge: Monochrome.
  - Try drawing this scene using only one gradient of color.

Did you know?

We also make books to help with storytelling. With help on things like creating characters, world-building, magic systems, and more!

You can find more information on our website, www.TCStudiosHQ.com.

#35 – Soft. (I) (P) (AP)

Brainstorm ...

- Fur.
- Fabric.
- People.
- Blanket.

Brainstorm ...

- Practice: Hair.
  - Study the flow and lighting dimensions of hair and implement the techniques into your drawing.

Drawing Exercise #7

Draw 10 items that are shiny.

\#36 – Shiny. (C) (I) (G)

Brainstorm …   42

- Is it someone's face?
- Is it an object?
  - Is it metal?
  - Is it glass?
  - Is it silver or gold?
- Is it in the sun, or under lights?

Brainstorm …

- Experiment: Colored Lighting.
  - When/if you are applying lighting effects to this piece, try using a different color instead of just a lighter gradient of the lit area.

Did you know?

We also publish novels and comics that you can read!

You can find more information on our website, www.TCStudiosHQ.com.

\#37 – Rough. (P) (AP) (W)

Brainstorm …

- Is this figurative or literal?
  - Is someone having a bad day?
  - Does someone have rough skin?
  - Is there a rough dirt road?
  - Is someone being roughed up?

Brainstorm …

- Practice: Hands.
  - Study up on some hand techniques and implement them in your drawing.
    - Maybe they're rubbing lotion into their hands or putting on a bandage.

Do you want to give us a prompt for next year's edition?

You can submit prompt ideas you have based on next year's chapter themes. Credit will be given if selected.

You can find more information on our website, www.TCStudiosHQ.com.

#38 – Fuzzy. (P) (G) (CP)

Brainstorm …

- Is it an animal?
- Is it someone's hair?
- Is it the texture of fabric?
- Is it being pet, cuddled or felt?

Brainstorm (Drawing) …

- Challenge: Opposite Colors.
    - Pick a color and its opposite (ex: red and green).
    - Try coloring this piece with only those two colors and their gradients.

Did you know?

We post daily writing & drawing prompts on our Social Medias for everyone to participate in.

Find us @PromptParty and use #PromptParty.

You can find more information on our website, www.TCStudiosHQ.com.

\#39 – Chiseled. (W) (I) (M)

Brainstorm …

- Is it someone's chin?
  - What other kind of bone structure might this person have?
- Is it stone?
  - Why is it being chiseled?
    - What might it look like when it's finished?
  - Was it found like that?

Brainstorm …

- Focus on: Body Language.
  - How can you position the body to emphasize this prompt?

Did you know?

In addition to posting daily on Social Media, we have daily interactive posts on our YouTube channel, Podcast, and Blog.

You can find more information on our website, www.TCStudiosHQ.com.

#40 – Slick. (P) (AP) (CP)

Brainstorm …

- Is this being used to describe an item or a person?
- How might a person with a slick personality look?
    - How would they act?
    - Can you capture this in your image?
- What are some items that are slick?
    - Soap? Grease? Mucus?

Brainstorm …

- Challenge: Continuous line.
    - Try drawing this scene with one continuous line.
    - You can color the finished image.

Drawing Exercise #8

Draw 10 things that are rigid.

#41 – Greasy. (I) (G) (W)

> ### *Brainstorm ...*
>
> - Is this figurative or literal?
> - How does a greasy person behave?
>   - What goes on in their day to day?
>   - How might they dress?
> - Where can you find grease?
>   - A mechanic shop.
>   - A barber shop.

> ### *Brainstorm ...*
>
> - Practice: Hair.
>   - Study the flow and lighting of hair and implement the techniques into your drawing.

Remember!

The listed genres/mediums and brainstorming boxes are **only suggestions!** We encourage you to do/use whatever you want.

47

\#42 – Toned. (C) (M) (AP)

<table>
<tr><td>

Brainstorm …

- Maybe show the process of someone trying to tone up their body.
    - Are they getting ready for summer?
    - Have they been bullied into change?

</td></tr>
</table>

<table>
<tr><td>

Brainstorm …

- Practice: Anatomy.
    - Study proportions, positioning, and structure techniques and implement them in your drawing.

</td></tr>
</table>

You can share your work with us on Facebook, Instagram & Twitter!

Tag us @PromptParty and use #PromptParty.

We'd love to see what you come up with!

\#43 – Cracked. (W) (P) (I)

Brainstorm …

- What cracked?
    - An egg?
    - Nail polish?
    - Skin?
    - The sidewalk?

Brainstorm …

- Challenge: No references.
    - Put your muscle memory to the test and draw this scene without using any references.
        - Good luck!

Do you want your work published?

You can submit any work made using our prompts to our annual anthologies! Published submissions receive shared 25% royalties.

You can find more information on our website, www.TCStudiosHQ.com.

\#44 – Smooth. (G) (C) (AP)

Brainstorm …

- A kitchen counter?
- Butter?
- A fresh jar of peanut butter?
- Someone's personality?
- The hood of a brand-new car?

Brainstorm …

- Challenge: Secondary Colors.
  - Try drawing this scene using only secondary colors and their gradients.

Did you know?

A percentage of every anthology sold goes towards helping communities like yours. This includes donations to charities, funding of scholarships, creating of programs, and more!

You can find more information on our website, www.TCStudiosHQ.com.

#45 – Scratchy. (CP) (M) (I)

Brainstorm ...

- A wool sweater?
- An annoyed cat?
- A pile of hay?
- Someone with chickenpox?

Brainstorm ...

- Experiment: Bold Line Work.
  - When you've finished lining your work (if you're lining), try making some areas thicker than others.
    - It can be dramatically, or just a bit.
      - Take note of how it changes the tone of your work.

Drawing Exercise #9

Draw 10 things that are soft.

#46 – Hairy. (W) (M) (P)

<table><tr><td>

Brainstorm …

- Someone's body?
- A dangerous situation?
- A monster?

</td></tr></table>

<table><tr><td>

Brainstorm …

- Life Study.
  - Go out and find a person with this prompt to sketch.
  - See if someone you know will let you draw them!

</td></tr></table>

Be The First To Know.

Join our newsletter and be the first to know about new prompt books, novels, comics, giveaways, freebies, coupons, and anything else we've got going on!

Find our newsletter on our website, www.TCStudiosHQ.com.

\#47 – Gooey. (I) (CP) (AP)

Brainstorm …

- Where do you find something that's gooey?
  - o   The swamp?
  - o   A sewer?
  - o   Your nose?

Brainstorm …

- Experiment: Comic Strip.
  - o   Try drawing this as a short comic strip.

Did you know?

In addition to our annual prompt anthologies, every year we have
<u>themed</u> anthologies that you can also submit to!

You can find more information on our website,
www.TCStudiosHQ.com.

#48 – Leathery. (M) (G) (C)

<table><tr><td>

Brainstorm ...

- Clothing?
- Furniture?
- Skin texture?

</td></tr></table>

<table><tr><td>

Brainstorm ...

- Challenge: Bird's Eye View.
  - Try drawing this piece with a bird's eye view.

</td></tr></table>

Looking for a challenge?

Try doing one of our prompts with your friend(s)! See if you can come up with something together.

54

#49 – Rubbery. (W) (AP) (I)

Brainstorm …

- What are some things that are rubbery?
    - o   What are they used for?
    - o   How can you get their stretchiness across in your image?

Brainstorm (Drawing) …

- Practice: Texture.
    - o   Study texture techniques and implement them in your drawing.

Did you know?

We also make books to help with storytelling. With help on things like creating characters, world-building, magic systems, and more!

You can find more information on our website,
www.TCStudiosHQ.com.

#50 – Metallic. (CP) (M) (G)

Brainstorm …

- A robotic limb?
- A metal button/pin?
- Stainless steel?
- Braces?
- A machine?

Brainstorm …

- Challenge: No Linework.
  - Try drawing this scene with no outlining – just dive right in with blocks of color!

Drawing Exercise #10

Draw 10 things that are stretchy.

#51 – Feathery. (AP) (C) (W)

Brainstorm …

- Birds?
- Feather quills?
- Is someone being tickled?
- A down feather pillow?

Brainstorm …

- Practice different types of shading techniques.
    - Hatching.
    - Cross-Hatching.
    - Stippling.
    - Scribbling.
    - Contour Lines.

Did you know?

We also publish novels and comics that you can read!

You can find more information on our website,
www.TCStudiosHQ.com.

\#52 – Jean. (I) (CP) (G)

<table>
<tr><td>

Brainstorm …

- Jacket?
- Pants?
- Accessories?
- How is it styled?
    - Are there pins?
    - Are there iron-on patches?
    - Is there any writing?
- How is it being worn?

</td></tr>
</table>

<table>
<tr><td>

Brainstorm …

- Challenge: Input.
    - Let someone tell you how you should set up your drawing and follow their instructions to the best of your ability.

</td></tr>
</table>

Do you want to give us a prompt for next year's edition?

You can submit prompt ideas you have based on next year's chapter themes. Credit will be given if selected.

You can find more information on our website, www.TCStudiosHQ.com.

\#53 – Cotton. (AP) (C) (M)

Brainstorm …

- Is it growing?
- Has it been made into something?
    - Clothing?
    - Furniture?

Brainstorm …

- Challenge: Monochrome.
    - Try drawing this scene using only one gradient of color.

Did you know?

We post daily writing & drawing prompts on our Social Medias for everyone to participate in.

Find us @PromptParty and use #PromptParty.

You can find more information on our website, www.TCStudiosHQ.com.

#54 – Stretchy. (CP) (G) (P)

Brainstorm …

- Gum?
- Leggings?
- How might the look of something change when it's being stretched?
- What's causing it to stretch?
    - Is it supposed to?

Brainstorm (Drawing) …

- Challenge: Opposite Colors.
    - Pick a color and it's opposite (ex: red and green).
    - Try coloring this piece with only those two colors and their gradients.

Did you know?

In addition to posting daily on Social Media, we have daily interactive posts on our YouTube channel, Podcast, and Blog.

You can find more information on our website, www.TCStudiosHQ.com.

#55 – Rigid.

Brainstorm …   61

- Is this figurative or literal?
  - Is it someone's point of view?
    - Their personality?
  - Is it something physical?
    - A wall?
    - A metal pole?

Brainstorm …

- Practice: Lighting.
  - Study color choice, gradients, and placement techniques of lighting and implement them in your drawing.

Drawing Exercise #11

Draw 10 things that are smooth.

#56 – Wooden. (P) (W) (C)

Brainstorm …

- What kind of wood?
    - Is it light or dark?
    - Is it dense or weak?
- How is it shown?
    - Naturally?
    - As furniture?
    - What condition is it in?

Brainstorm …

- Challenge: Continuous line.
    - Try drawing this scene with one continuous line.
    - You can color the finished image.

Remember!

The listed genres/mediums and brainstorming boxes are **only suggestions!** We encourage you to do/use whatever you want.

\#57 – Glass. (M) (AP) (I)

Brainstorm …

- What kind of glass?
  - Clear?
  - Stained?
  - Foggy?
- How is it made?
  - Is it a cup?
  - Is it a jar?
  - Is it a bowl?

Brainstorm …

- Challenge: Self-Portrait.
  - Draw yourself into this scene.

You can share your work with us on Facebook, Instagram & Twitter!

Tag us @PromptParty and use #PromptParty.

We'd love to see what you come up with!

\#58 – Plastic. (CP) (G) (C)

<table>
<tr><td>

Brainstorm …

- What is it being used for?
- What color is it?
- Is it BPA free?

</td></tr>
</table>

<table>
<tr><td>

Brainstorm …

- Challenge: Secondary Colors.
  - Try drawing this scene using only secondary colors and their gradients.

</td></tr>
</table>

Do you want your work published?

You can submit any work made using our prompts to our annual anthologies! Published submissions receive shared 25% royalties.

You can find more information on our website, www.TCStudiosHQ.com.

#59 – Silicone. (P) (AP) (W)

Brainstorm ...

- What is it being used for?
  - Food?
  - Body enhancements?

Brainstorm ...

- Experiment: Exaggerated Proportions/Features.
  - Get a little cartoony.
  - How might exaggerating certain features help the imagery?

Did you know?

A percentage of every anthology sold goes towards helping communities like yours. This includes donations to charities, funding of scholarships, creating of programs, and more!

You can find more information on our website, www.TCStudiosHQ.com.

#60 – Canvas. (P) (I) (W)

Brainstorm ...   66

- What is it being used for?
  - Painting?
  - Fashion accessory?
- What color is it?
- What quality is it?
- What condition is it in?

Brainstorm ...

- Experiment: Comic Strip.
  - Try drawing this as a short comic strip.

Drawing Exercise #12

Draw 10 things that are fuzzy.

Chapter Three: Poses.

#61 – Sitting. (C) (AP) (M)

Brainstorm …

- Where?
    - Sofa?
    - Chair?
    - Bed?
    - Floor?
- How?
    - Legs crossed?
    - Legs folded?
    - Feet up?
- What's their mood?
    - Tired?
    - Calm?
    - Anxious?

Brainstorm …

- Challenge: Color Palette.
    - Use a random color palette generator or ask a friend to pick 3-5 colors for you to use.

Did you know?

In addition to our annual prompt anthologies, every year we have <u>themed</u> anthologies that you can also submit to!

You can find more information on our website,
www.TCStudiosHQ.com.

#62 – Sleeping. (G) (I) (CP)

Brainstorm ...

- Where?
    - Car?
    - Bed?
    - Crib?
    - Sofa?
- How?
    - Soundly?
    - Restlessly?
    - Sleep walking?

Brainstorm ...

- Challenge: No references.
    - Put your muscle memory to the test and draw this scene without using any references.
        - Good luck!

Looking for a challenge?

Try doing one of our prompts with your friend(s)! See if you can come up with something together.

\#63 – Jumping. (W) (CP) (I)

Brainstorm …

69

- Why?
    - For joy?
    - For exercise?
    - To play?
    - To avoid something?
- How?
    - Carefully?
    - Haphazardly?
    - Wildly?

Brainstorm …

- Experiment: Bold Line Work.
    - When you've finished lining your work (if you're lining), try making some areas thicker than others.
        - It can be dramatically, or just a bit.
            - Take note of how it changes the tone of your work.

Did you know?

We also make books to help with storytelling. With help on things like creating characters, world-building, magic systems, and more!

You can find more information on our website,
www.TCStudiosHQ.com.

#64 – Stretching. (M) (AP) (G)

Brainstorm …

- What's being stretched?
  - Someone's body?
  - Fabric?
  - Rubber?
  - Someone's patience?
- Why?
  - Preparing for a workout?
  - Creating clothing?
  - Being stressed out?

Brainstorm …

- Focus on: Body Language.
  - How can you position the body to emphasize this prompt?

Did you know?

We also publish novels and comics that you can read!

You can find more information on our website,
www.TCStudiosHQ.com.

#65 – Pin-up. (P) (C) (AP)

Brainstorm ...

- What are they wearing?
- How are they posed?
- How is their hair styled?
- Are there any props?

Brainstorm ...

- Challenge: Monochrome.
  - o Try drawing this scene using only one gradient of color.

Drawing Exercise #13

Draw someone posing for a professional photoshoot.

#66 – Crawling. (I) (W) (M)

Brainstorm ...

- Who?
    - An adult?
    - A baby?
    - An animal?
- Why?
    - Are they unable to walk?
    - Sneaking?
    - Training?

Brainstorm (Drawing) ...

- Challenge: Opposite Colors.
    - Pick a color and it's opposite (ex: red and green).
    - Try coloring this piece with only those two colors and their gradients.

Do you want to give us a prompt for next year's edition?

You can submit prompt ideas you have based on next year's chapter themes. Credit will be given if selected.

You can find more information on our website, www.TCStudiosHQ.com.

#67 – Break Dancing. (G) (P) (I)

> ***Brainstorm …***
>
> - What genre of music are they dancing to?
> - Are they dancing alone or with a group?
> - Is it choreographed or freestyled?
> - Where are they?
>   - On the street?
>   - In a garage?
>   - In a dance studio?
> - What are their outfits like?
> - Are they good at the breakdancing or do they need to practice?

> ***Brainstorm …***
>
> - Experiment: Colored Lighting.
>   - When/if you are applying lighting effects to this piece, try using a different color instead of just a lighter gradient of the lit area.

Did you know?

We post daily writing & drawing prompts on our Social Medias for everyone to participate in.

Find us @PromptParty and use #PromptParty.

You can find more information on our website, www.TCStudiosHQ.com.

#68 – Salsa Dancing. (AP) (M) (C)

Brainstorm ...

- Are they practicing or preforming?
- Are they solo or with a partner?
- What kind of outfit are they wearing?

Brainstorm ...

- Practice: Anatomy.
    - Study proportions, positioning, and structure techniques and implement them in your drawing.

Did you know?

In addition to posting daily on Social Media, we have daily interactive posts on our YouTube channel, Podcast, and Blog.

You can find more information on our website, www.TCStudiosHQ.com.

#69 – Sliding. (G) (W) (CP)

Brainstorm …

- How?
  - On their feet on a wet surface?
  - On their bum on a water slide?
- How do they feel about it?
  - Are they enjoying themselves?
  - Are they scared?
  - Are they confused?

Brainstorm …

- Challenge: Bird's Eye View.
  - Try drawing this piece with a bird's eye view.

Remember!

The listed genres/mediums and brainstorming boxes are **only suggestions!** We encourage you to do/use whatever you want.

#70 – Jumping Jacks. (AP) (I) (M)

Brainstorm …

- Why?
    - For exercise?
    - For training?
    - Are they being forced to or is this part of their routine?

Brainstorm …

- Challenge: No Linework.
    - Try drawing this scene with no outlining – just dive right in with blocks of color!

Drawing Exercise #14

Draw someone's reaction to being scared.

#71 – Running. (C) (W) (I)

Brainstorm ...

- Why?
  - Exercise?
  - Training?
  - Running away from danger?
  - Running towards danger?
  - Chasing a criminal?
- What is their form like?
  - Is it good?
  - Is it wild?
  - Is it lazy?

Brainstorm ...

- Experiment: Exaggerated Proportions/Features.
  - Get a little cartoony.
  - How might exaggerating certain features help the imagery?

Be The First To Know.

Join our newsletter and be the first to know about new prompt books, novels, comics, giveaways, freebies, coupons, and anything else we've got going on!

Find our newsletter on our website, www.TCStudiosHQ.com.

\#72 – Spinning. (G) (M) (AP)

Brainstorm …

- What is spinning?
    - A person?
    - A toy?
    - Someone's thoughts?
    - The sky?
        - Play around with how you can *spin* this.

Brainstorm …

- Challenge: Continuous line.
    - Try drawing this scene with one continuous line.
    - You can color the finished image.

You can share your work with us on Facebook, Instagram & Twitter!

Tag us @PromptParty and use #PromptParty.

We'd love to see what you come up with!

#73 – Sneaking. (P) (CP) (W)

Brainstorm …

- Why?
    - Are they afraid of getting caught?
    - Are they trying to be quiet?
    - Are they trying to steal/eavesdrop something?
- Are they good or bad at it?
- What happens if they get caught?
    - Does it matter?

Brainstorm …

- Experiment: Comic Strip.
    - Try drawing this as a short comic strip.

Do you want your work published?

You can submit any work made using our prompts to our annual anthologies! Published submissions receive shared 25% royalties.

You can find more information on our website,
www.TCStudiosHQ.com.

#74 – Walking. (M) (I) (G)

Brainstorm …   80

- Where?
    - In the park?
    - To the bus stop?
    - On the sidewalk?
    - On a treadmill?
- With who?
    - Themselves?
    - Their partner?
    - Their dog?
    - Their kid(s)?
    - A friend?

Brainstorm …

- Focus on: Storyline.
    - Can you tell a story using this prompt?

Did you know?

A percentage of every anthology sold goes towards helping communities like yours. This includes donations to charities, funding of scholarships, creating of programs, and more!

You can find more information on our website, www.TCStudiosHQ.com.

#75 – Kissing. (G) (AP) (P)

Brainstorm …

- Who?
    - o A lover?
    - o A friend?
    - o A child?
    - o A pet?
    - o A family member?
- How?
    - o Tenderly?
    - o Happily?
    - o Passionately?
    - o Sadly?

Brainstorm …

- Practice: Hands.
    - o Study up on some hand techniques and implement them in your drawing.
        - ▪ Maybe they're holding onto someone's face or shoulders.

Drawing Exercise #15

Draw a dog ready to play.

\#76 – Rolling. (W) (M) (CP)

Brainstorm …

- How is this interpreted?
  - Is someone rolling on the floor?
    - Why? Are they on fire?
    - Are they rolling down a hill?
  - Is a ball of dough being rolled out?
  - Is a piece of paper being rolled up?

Brainstorm …

- Challenge: Secondary Colors.
  - Try drawing this scene using only secondary colors and their gradients.

Did you know?

In addition to our annual prompt anthologies, every year we have <u>themed</u> anthologies that you can also submit to!

You can find more information on our website, www.TCStudiosHQ.com.

#77 – Playing. (I) (P) (W)

Brainstorm ...

- Playing what?
    - o A game?
    - o A song?
    - o A movie?

Brainstorm ...

- Focus on: Background.
    - o Tell the story with the use of the background and its environment. Think about the use and placement of specific items to help get the point across.

Looking for a challenge?

Try doing one of our prompts with your friend(s)! See if you can come up with something together.

#78 – Laying. (C) (AP) (G)

Brainstorm ...

- Where?
    - In bed?
    - On a sofa?
    - On the floor?
- Why?
    - Are they sleeping?
    - Have they passed out?
    - Are they in pain?

Brainstorm ...

- Challenge: Continuous line.
    - Try drawing this scene with one continuous line.
    - You can color the finished image.

Did you know?

We also make books to help with storytelling. With help on things like creating characters, world-building, magic systems, and more!

You can find more information on our website, www.TCStudiosHQ.com.

#79 – Standing. (P) (M) (CP)

Brainstorm ...   85

- Where?
    - Waiting in line?
    - Waiting for the bus?
    - At work?
- How?
    - Impatiently?
    - Calmly?
    - Anxiously?

Brainstorm ...

- Life Study.
    - Go out and find a person with this prompt to sketch.
    - See if someone you know will let you draw them!

Did you know?

We also publish novels and comics that you can read!

You can find more information on our website,
www.TCStudiosHQ.com.

#80 – Crouching. (I) (G) (W)

<table>
<tr><td>

Brainstorm ...

- Why?
    - o   Are they hiding?
    - o   Are they getting ready to attack?
    - o   Are they in pain?

</td></tr>
</table>

<table>
<tr><td>

Brainstorm ...

- Challenge: Monochrome.
    - o   Try drawing this scene using only one gradient of color.

</td></tr>
</table>

Drawing Exercise #16

Draw someone who is ready to fight.

#81 – Punching. (C) (G) (AP)

Brainstorm …

- What's being punched?
  - A person?
  - A punching bag?
  - A wall?
- Why?
  - During a fight?
  - Out of rage?
  - To train?

Brainstorm …

- Practice different types of shading techniques.
  - Hatching.
  - Cross-Hatching.
  - Stippling.
  - Scribbling.
  - Contour Lines.

Do you want to give us a prompt for next year's edition?

You can submit prompt ideas you have based on next year's chapter themes. Credit will be given if selected.

You can find more information on our website, www.TCStudiosHQ.com.

#82 – Kicking. (CP) (W) (M)

Brainstorm ...   88

- What's being kicked?
  - A person?
    - Why?
  - A ball?
  - An object?
    - Why?
- How is it being kicked?
  - Is the person aiming?
  - Is it an accident?
  - Are their movements wild?

Brainstorm ...

- Challenge: Input.
  - Let someone tell you how you should set up your drawing and follow their instructions to the best of your ability.

Did you know?

We post daily writing & drawing prompts on our Social Medias for everyone to participate in.

Find us @PromptParty and use #PromptParty.

You can find more information on our website, www.TCStudiosHQ.com.

#83 – Tiptoeing. (P) (AP) (CP)

Brainstorm …

- With shoes? Without shoes?
- Why?
    - Trying to be quiet?
    - Trying to stay hidden?

Brainstorm …

- Focus on: Body Language.
    - How can you position the body to emphasize this prompt?

Did you know?

In addition to posting daily on Social Media, we have daily interactive posts on our YouTube channel, Podcast, and Blog.

You can find more information on our website, www.TCStudiosHQ.com.

#84 – Licking. (W) (I) (G)

Brainstorm …

- Ice cream?
- Lips?
- A stamp?
- An envelope?

Brainstorm …

- Challenge: Self-Portrait.
  - Draw yourself into this scene.

Remember!

The listed genres/mediums and brainstorming boxes are **only suggestions!** We encourage you to do/use whatever you want.

#85 – Hiding. (W) (M) (AP)

Brainstorm …

- From who/what?
- Why?
- Are they doing it well?
- What are they using to hide?
- How long do they need to stay hidden?

Brainstorm (Drawing) …

- Practice: Texture.
    - Study texture techniques and implement them in your drawing.

Drawing Exercise #17

Draw someone pretending to be surprised.

\#86 – Blocking. (CP) (I) (G)

Brainstorm …

- What's being blocked?
    - o A punch/kick?
    - o A cellular signal?
    - o A radio signal?
    - o Another form of attack?

Brainstorm …

- Experiment: Bold Line Work.
    - o When you've finished lining your work (if you're lining), try making some areas thicker than others.
        - ▪ It can be dramatically, or just a bit.
            - • Take note of how it changes the tone of your work.

Be The First To Know.

Join our newsletter and be the first to know about new prompt books, novels, comics, giveaways, freebies, coupons, and anything else we've got going on!

Find our newsletter on our website, www.TCStudiosHQ.com.

\#87 – Fighting. (P) (G) (M)

<table>
<tr><td>

Brainstorm …

- Who is fighting?
- Why?
- Where?
- How?

</td></tr>
</table>

<table>
<tr><td>

Brainstorm …

- Practice: Anatomy.
  - Study proportions, positioning, and structure techniques and implement them in your drawing.

</td></tr>
</table>

You can share your work with us on Facebook, Instagram & Twitter!

Tag us @PromptParty and use #PromptParty.

We'd love to see what you come up with!

#88 – Praying. (I) (CP) (C)

Brainstorm …

- Who is praying?
- What are they praying about?
- Who are they praying to?
- Have they done so before?
    - If not, why start now?

Brainstorm …

- Challenge: Monochrome.
    - Try drawing this scene using only one gradient of color.

Do you want your work published?

You can submit any work made using our prompts to our annual anthologies! Published submissions receive shared 25% royalties.

You can find more information on our website,
www.TCStudiosHQ.com.

#89 – Hugging. (AP) (W) (G)

Brainstorm ...

- Who is being hugged?
    - A person?
    - An animal?
    - A tree?
- Why?
- How is it being done?
    - Happily?
    - Sadly?
    - Thankfully?

Brainstorm ...

- Challenge: No references.
    - Put your muscle memory to the test and draw this scene without using any references.
        - Good luck!

Did you know?

A percentage of every anthology sold goes towards helping communities like yours. This includes donations to charities, funding of scholarships, creating of programs, and more!

You can find more information on our website, www.TCStudiosHQ.com.

\#90 – Pointing. (C) (I) (M)

__Brainstorm ...__   96

- What is pointing?
    - Someone's finger?
    - A sign?
    - An arrow?
- What is it pointing at?
- Why is something/someone being pointed at?

__Brainstorm ...__

- Challenge: Bird's Eye View.
    - Try drawing this piece with a bird's eye view.

Drawing Exercise #18

Draw someone posing to admire their muscles.

#91 – Waving. (CP) (I) (W)

Brainstorm …

- What is waving?
  - o Someone's hand?
  - o A flag?
- Why?
  - o Wind?
  - o Saying hello or goodbye?

Brainstorm (Drawing) …

- Challenge: Opposite Colors.
  - o Pick a color and it's opposite (ex: red and green).
  - o Try coloring this piece with only those two colors and their gradients.

Did you know?

In addition to our annual prompt anthologies, every year we have themed anthologies that you can also submit to!

You can find more information on our website, www.TCStudiosHQ.com.

Chapter Four: Animals.

#92 – Snake. (CP) (AP) (G)

Brainstorm ...

- What kind of snake?
- How big is it?
- Where is it?
- Is it hunting?
- What is it doing?

Brainstorm ...

- Challenge: Color Palette.
  - Use a random color palette generator or ask a friend to pick 3-5 colors for you to use.

Looking for a challenge?

Try doing one of our prompts with your friend(s)! See if you can come up with something together.

\#93 – Turtle. (I) (P) (C)

<table>
<tr><td>

Brainstorm ...

- What kind of turtle?
- Where is it?
- Is it hiding?
- Is it alone?
- Is it racing a hare?

</td></tr>
</table>

<table>
<tr><td>

Brainstorm ...

- Challenge: No Linework.
  - Try drawing this scene with no outlining – just dive right in with blocks of color!

</td></tr>
</table>

Did you know?

We also make books to help with storytelling. With help on things like creating characters, world-building, magic systems, and more!

You can find more information on our website,
www.TCStudiosHQ.com.

\#94 – Pig. (M) (W) (CP)

Brainstorm …

- How big is it?
- What color is it?
- What is it doing?
- Is it covered in mud?
- Is this a metaphor for a person?

Brainstorm …

- Challenge: Continuous line.
    o   Try drawing this scene with one continuous line.
    o   You can color the finished image.

Did you know?

We also publish novels and comics that you can read!

You can find more information on our website,
www.TCStudiosHQ.com.

#95 – Rabbit. (AP) (I) (G)

Brainstorm ...

- What color is it?
- Is it alone?
- Is it hopping?
- Is it eating something?
- Is it racing a tortoise?

Brainstorm ...

- Experiment: Comic Strip.
  - Try drawing this as a short comic strip.

Drawing Exercise #19

Draw 5 different types of birds.

\#96 – Dog. (G) (W) (M)

Brainstorm …

- What kind of dog?
- Is it friendly or aggressive?
- Does it have a service job?
- How old is it?
- Does it like to play?
    - Does it prefer to sleep?

Brainstorm …

- Practice: Hair.
    - Study the flow and lighting dimensions of hair and implement the techniques into your drawing.

Do you want to give us a prompt for next year's edition?

You can submit prompt ideas you have based on next year's chapter themes. Credit will be given if selected.

You can find more information on our website, www.TCStudiosHQ.com.

\#97 – Chicken. (P) (I) (AP)

Brainstorm …

- What color is it?
- What is it doing?
- Does it have any chicks?
- Has it lain any eggs?

Brainstorm (Drawing) …

- Practice: Texture.
    - Study texture techniques and implement them in your drawing.

Did you know?

We post daily writing & drawing prompts on our Social Medias for everyone to participate in.

Find us @PromptParty and use #PromptParty.

You can find more information on our website, www.TCStudiosHQ.com.

#98 – Dragon. (CP) (W) (M)

Brainstorm ...

- What kind?
- What color is it?
- How big is it?
- Is it tamed or wild?
- Is it friendly or aggressive?

Brainstorm ...

- Experiment: Colored Lighting.
  - When/if you are applying lighting effects to this piece, try using a different color instead of just a lighter gradient of the lit area.

Remember!

The listed genres/mediums and brainstorming boxes are **only suggestions!** We encourage you to do/use whatever you want.

\#99 – Frog. (I) (AP) (G)

Brainstorm …

- What kind?
- Where is it?
- Is it a pet?
- An experiment?

Brainstorm (Drawing) …

- Challenge: Opposite Colors.
  - Pick a color and it's opposite (ex: red and green).
  - Try coloring this piece with only those two colors and their gradients.

You can share your work with us on Facebook, Instagram & Twitter!

Tag us @PromptParty and use #PromptParty.

We'd love to see what you come up with!

\#100 – Sheep. (W) (AP) (M)

Brainstorm ...

- How many are there?
- What color is the wool?
- Does it have any wool?
    - Has it just been shaved?
- Is there a shepherd?
- Is there a dog to heard them?

Brainstorm ...

- Challenge: Continuous line.
    - Try drawing this scene with one continuous line.
    - You can color the finished image.

Drawing Exercise #20

Draw 5 different animals sleeping.

\#101 – Wolf. (I) (P) (G)

Brainstorm …

- Is it alone or in a pack?
- Is it hunting?
- Is it howling?
- Where is it?

Brainstorm …

- Practice: Lighting.
    - Study color choice, gradients, and placement techniques of lighting and implement them in your drawing.

Do you want your work published?

You can submit any work made using our prompts to our annual anthologies! Published submissions receive shared 25% royalties.

You can find more information on our website, www.TCStudiosHQ.com.

#102 – Mermaid. (W) (CP) (G)

Brainstorm …

- What colors make up its design?
- Is it more human or more fish?
- How old is it?
- What is it doing?

Brainstorm …

- Challenge: No references.
  - Put your muscle memory to the test and draw this scene without using any references.
    - Good luck!

Did you know?

A percentage of every anthology sold goes towards helping communities like yours. This includes donations to charities, funding of scholarships, creating of programs, and more!

You can find more information on our website, www.TCStudiosHQ.com.

\#103 – Whale. (AP) (P) (I)

Brainstorm …

- Was it spotted out at sea? On a beach?
- Is it alone or with a group?
- Is it coming up for air?
- Is it splashing the water with its tail?

Brainstorm …

- Challenge: Bird's Eye View.
    - Try drawing this piece with a bird's eye view.

Did you know?

In addition to our annual prompt anthologies, every year we have
themed anthologies that you can also submit to!

You can find more information on our website,
www.TCStudiosHQ.com.

#104 – Wild Cat. (M) (W) (CP)

Brainstorm …

- What kind?
- Is it hunting?
- Is it alone?
- What is its habitat like?
- Does it have a pattern on its fur?

Brainstorm …

- Challenge: Secondary Colors.
  - Try drawing this scene using only secondary colors and their gradients.

Looking for a challenge?

Try doing one of our prompts with your friend(s)! See if you can come up with something together.

#105 – Elephant. (I) (C) (AP)

Brainstorm …

- Male or female?
  - If male, are its tusks intact?
    - How big are they?
  - If female, does it have a child?
    - Are they traveling as a family?
- What are they doing?

Brainstorm …

- Challenge: Input.
  - Let someone tell you how you should set up your drawing and follow their instructions to the best of your ability.

Drawing Exercise #21

Draw 5 different types of dogs.

#106 – Polar Bear. (G) (AP) (M)

Brainstorm …

- What is it doing?
- Is it fishing?
- Does it have cubs?

Brainstorm …

- Challenge: No Linework.
    - Try drawing this scene with no outlining – just dive right in with blocks of color!

Did you know?

We also make books to help with storytelling. With help on things like creating characters, world-building, magic systems, and more!

You can find more information on our website, www.TCStudiosHQ.com.

\#107 – Fox. (W) (CP) (C)

Brainstorm ...

- What color is it?
- What is it doing?
- Is it alone?
- Is it hunting?

Brainstorm ...

- Practice: Hair.
  - Study the flow and lighting of hair and implement the techniques into your drawing.

Did you know?

We also publish novels and comics that you can read!

You can find more information on our website,
www.TCStudiosHQ.com.

#108 – Extinct Animal. (I) (G) (M)

Brainstorm …

- Which one?
- Why did it go extinct?
- What were its mannerisms?
- Where did it live?
- What did it eat?

Brainstorm …

- Challenge: Monochrome.
  - Try drawing this scene using only one gradient of color.

Do you want to give us a prompt for next year's edition?

You can submit prompt ideas you have based on next year's chapter themes. Credit will be given if selected.

You can find more information on our website, www.TCStudiosHQ.com.

#109 – Phoenix. (AP) (P) (W)

Brainstorm …

- Has it risen from the ashes?
- How big is it?
- What is it doing?

Brainstorm …

- Focus on: Storyline.
    - Can you tell a story using this prompt?

Did you know?

We post daily writing & drawing prompts on our Social Medias for everyone to participate in.

Find us @PromptParty and use #PromptParty.

You can find more information on our website, www.TCStudiosHQ.com.

#110 – Crab. (C) (AP) (G)

Brainstorm …

- What kind?
- Where is it?
- What is it doing?

Brainstorm …

- Experiment: Bold Line Work.
  - When you've finished lining your work (if you're lining), try making some areas thicker than others.
    - It can be dramatically, or just a bit.
      - Take note of how it changes the tone of your work.

Drawing Exercise #22

Draw 5 different animals attacking.

\#111 – Hummingbird. (CP) (W) (P)

Brainstorm …

- What color is it?
- What is it doing?
  - Is it flying?
  - Is it drinking?
- Where is it?

Brainstorm …

- Challenge: Life Reference.
  - See if you can take your own reference photos to use in your drawing.

Did you know?

In addition to posting daily on Social Media, we have daily interactive posts on our YouTube channel, Podcast, and Blog.

You can find more information on our website, www.TCStudiosHQ.com.

#112 – Cat. (CP) (W) (M)

Brainstorm ...

- What color is it?
- What is it doing?
    - Cuddling?
    - Sleeping?
    - Cleaning itself?
    - Playing?
- Does it have any interesting features?

Brainstorm ...

- Life Study.
    - Go out and find a cat to sketch.
    - See if someone you know will let you draw their cat!

Remember!

The listed genres/mediums and brainstorming boxes are **only suggestions!** We encourage you to do/use whatever you want.

\#113 – Dolphin. (I) (AP) (G)

Brainstorm …

- What is it doing?
    - o Doing flips?
    - o Playing with a human?
    - o Coming up for air?
- Is it alone?
- Where is it?

Brainstorm …

- Focus on: Realism.
    - o Try making the subject material for this prompt look as realistic as you can.

Be The First To Know.

Join our newsletter and be the first to know about new prompt books, novels, comics, giveaways, freebies, coupons, and anything else we've got going on!

Find our newsletter on our website, www.TCStudiosHQ.com.

\#114 – Monkey. (P) (C) (W)

Brainstorm ...

- What kind?
  - What color is it?
  - Does it have a pattern?
- What is it doing?
- Is it alone?
- Is it docile or aggressive?

Brainstorm ...

- Practice: Hands.
  - Study up on some hand techniques and implement them in your drawing.
    - Maybe they're holding a banana or picking bugs out of their fur.

You can share your work with us on Facebook, Instagram & Twitter!

Tag us @PromptParty and use #PromptParty.

We'd love to see what you come up with!

\#115 – Reptile. (I) (AP) (G)

Brainstorm ...

- What kind?
  - What color is it?
  - Where does it live?
- What is it doing?
  - Eating?
  - Hiding?
  - Sunbathing?

Brainstorm ...

- Challenge: Continuous line.
  - Try drawing this scene with one continuous line.
  - You can color the finished image.

Drawing Exercise #23

Draw 5 different types of cats.

\#116 – Fish. (CP) (M) (C)

Brainstorm ...   122

- What kind?
  - What color is it?
  - Is it carnivorous?
  - Does it swim in a school?
  - Where does it live?
  - How deep can it go?

Brainstorm ...

- Challenge: No Linework.
  - Try drawing this scene with no outlining – just dive right in with blocks of color!

Do you want your work published?

You can submit any work made using our prompts to our annual anthologies! Published submissions receive shared 25% royalties.

You can find more information on our website, www.TCStudiosHQ.com.

\#117 – Goat. (P) (G) (W)

Brainstorm …

- What color is it?
- Where does it live?
- What is it doing?
- Is it docile or aggressive?

Brainstorm …

- Practice: Hair.
   - Study the flow and lighting of hair and implement the techniques into your drawing.

Did you know?

A percentage of every anthology sold goes towards helping communities like yours. This includes donations to charities, funding of scholarships, creating of programs, and more!

You can find more information on our website, www.TCStudiosHQ.com.

#118 – Deer. (AP) (I) (CP)

Brainstorm …

- Is it in the road?
- Is it being hunted?
- What is it doing?
- Is it alone?

Brainstorm …

- Practice different types of shading techniques.
    - Hatching.
    - Cross-Hatching.
    - Stippling.
    - Scribbling.
    - Contour Lines.

Did you know?

In addition to our annual prompt anthologies, every year we have
<u>themed</u> anthologies that you can also submit to!

You can find more information on our website,
www.TCStudiosHQ.com.

#119 – Shark. (G) (M) (C)

Brainstorm …

- What kind?
  - What is its shape like?
  - Does it have any patterns?
- Where is it?
- What is it doing?

Brainstorm …

- Experiment: Colored Lighting.
  - When/if you are applying lighting effects to this piece, try using a different color instead of just a lighter gradient of the lit area.

Looking for a challenge?

Try doing one of our prompts with your friend(s)! See if you can come up with something together.

#120 – Chipmunk. (P) (G) (AP)

Brainstorm ...

- What is it doing?
  - Eating?
  - Running?
- Where is it?
- Is it alone?

Brainstorm ...

- Experiment: Exaggerated Proportions/Features.
  - Get a little cartoony.
  - How might exaggerating certain features help the imagery?

Drawing Exercise #24

Draw 5 different animals playing.

#121 – Raccoon. (CP) (W) (M)

Brainstorm ...

- Where is it?
- What is it doing?
    - Sneaking around?
    - Eating?
    - Fighting?

Brainstorm ...

- Experiment: Comic Strip.
    - Try drawing this as a short comic strip.

Did you know?

We also make books to help with storytelling. With help on things like creating characters, world-building, magic systems, and more!

You can find more information on our website,
www.TCStudiosHQ.com.

Chapter Five: Plants.

#122 – Sunflower. (I) (AP) (M)

<table><tr><td>

Brainstorm …

- Where is it?
- Is it potted?
- What condition is it in?

</td></tr></table>

<table><tr><td>

Brainstorm …

- Challenge: Self-Portrait.
  - Draw yourself into this scene.

</td></tr></table>

Did you know?

We also publish novels and comics that you can read!

You can find more information on our website,
www.TCStudiosHQ.com.

\#123 – Daisy. (G) (W) (CP)

Brainstorm …

- What color is it?
- Where is it?
- What condition is it in?

Brainstorm …

- Challenge: No Linework.
    - Try drawing this scene with no outlining – just dive right in with blocks of color!

Do you want to give us a prompt for next year's edition?

You can submit prompt ideas you have based on next year's chapter themes. Credit will be given if selected.

You can find more information on our website, www.TCStudiosHQ.com.

\#124 – Pumpkin. (C) (P) (G)

Brainstorm …

- How big is it?
- Is it carved?
- Is it made into something?

Brainstorm …

- Focus on: Background.
  - Tell the story with the use of the background and its environment. Think about the use and placement of specific items to help get the point across.

Did you know?

We post daily writing & drawing prompts on our Social Medias for everyone to participate in.

Find us @PromptParty and use #PromptParty.

You can find more information on our website,
www.TCStudiosHQ.com.

#125 – Cactus. (AP) (W) (I)

Brainstorm ...

- Is it potted?
- Is it in the desert?
- Are there flowers?
- How big are the thorns?
- How big is the cactus?

Brainstorm (Drawing) ...

- Practice: Texture.
    - Study texture techniques and implement them in your drawing.

Drawing Exercise #25

Draw a plant during three different stages of growth.

131

#126 – Basil. (CP) (I) (M)

Brainstorm …

- What kind?
- How tall is it?
- What condition is it in?
- Is it being used to make something?
- What do the leaves look like?

Brainstorm …

- Challenge: Continuous line.
    - Try drawing this scene with one continuous line.
    - You can color the finished image.

Did you know?

In addition to posting daily on Social Media, we have daily interactive posts on our YouTube channel, Podcast, and Blog.

You can find more information on our website,
www.TCStudiosHQ.com.

\#127 – Jasmine. (AP) (G) (P)

Brainstorm ...

- Is it potted?
- Where is it?
- What's around it?
  - How can you complement its colors?

Brainstorm ...

- Challenge: Bird's Eye View.
  - Try drawing this piece with a bird's eye view.

Remember!

The listed genres/mediums and brainstorming boxes are **only suggestions!** We encourage you to do/use whatever you want.

#128 – Rose. (G) (CP) (M)

Brainstorm …

- What color is it?
- Is it a single rose or a bouquet?
  - Is it in a bush?
- Does it have thorns?
- Are the petals spread out or close together?

Brainstorm …

- Challenge: No references.
  - Put your muscle memory to the test and draw this scene without using any references.
    - Good luck!

Be The First To Know.

Join our newsletter and be the first to know about new prompt books, novels, comics, giveaways, freebies, coupons, and anything else we've got going on!

Find our newsletter on our website, www.TCStudiosHQ.com.

#129 – Mint. (W) (I) (AP)

<table><tr><td>

Brainstorm …

- Is it potted?
- What kind of mint is it?
- Is it being used for anything?

</td></tr></table>

<table><tr><td>

Brainstorm …

- Practice: Lighting.
  - Study color choice, gradients, and placement techniques of lighting and implement them in your drawing.

</td></tr></table>

You can share your work with us on Facebook, Instagram & Twitter!

Tag us @PromptParty and use #PromptParty.

We'd love to see what you come up with!

#130 – Vines. (P) (M) (C)

Brainstorm ...

- Are they long?
- Are they hanging from trees?
- Do they have thorns?
- What color are they?

Brainstorm ...

- Experiment: Bold Line Work.
  - When you've finished lining your work (if you're lining), try making some areas thicker than others.
    - It can be dramatically, or just a bit.
      - Take note of how it changes the tone of your work.

Drawing Exercise #26

Draw a plant that is wilting.

\#131 – Spinach. (AP) (G) (I)

Brainstorm …

- Where is it being grown?
  - On a farm?
  - In a garden?
- Is it being prepared?
- Is it being eaten?

Brainstorm …

- Challenge: Input.
  - Let someone tell you how you should set up your drawing and follow their instructions to the best of your ability.

Do you want your work published?

You can submit any work made using our prompts to our annual anthologies! Published submissions receive shared 25% royalties.

You can find more information on our website,
www.TCStudiosHQ.com.

#132 – Rubber Plant. (W) (G) (P)

Brainstorm …

- How big is it?
- Is it potted?
- Where is it?
- Is it in the sun?

Brainstorm …

- Focus on: Realism.
  - Try making the subject material for this prompt look as realistic as you can.

Did you know?

A percentage of every anthology sold goes towards helping communities like yours. This includes donations to charities, funding of scholarships, creating of programs, and more!

You can find more information on our website, www.TCStudiosHQ.com.

\#133 – Snake Plant. (AP) (I) (M)

Brainstorm ...

- Is it potted?
- How tall is it?
- Is it in the sun or shade?
- Is it with other plants?

Brainstorm ...

- Challenge: Secondary Colors.
    - Try drawing this scene using only secondary colors and their gradients.

Did you know?

In addition to our annual prompt anthologies, every year we have
<u>themed</u> anthologies that you can also submit to!

You can find more information on our website,
www.TCStudiosHQ.com.

\#134 – Orchid. (G) (C) (I)

Brainstorm ...

- What color is it?
- Is it potted?
  - What kind of pot is it in?
- Is it being given as a gift?

Brainstorm ...

- Challenge: Continuous line.
  - Try drawing this scene with one continuous line.
  - You can color the finished image.

Looking for a challenge?

Try doing one of our prompts with your friend(s)! See if you can
come up with something together.

\#135 – Tulip. (AP) (M) (CP)

Brainstorm …   141

- What color is it?
- Is it in a bouquet?
- What condition is it in?
- What are the petals like?

Brainstorm …

- Challenge: Life Reference.
    - See if you can take your own reference photos to use in your drawing.

Drawing Exercise #27

Draw a garden of your favorite fruit/vegetables.

141

#136 – Sakura. (CP) (AP) (I)

Brainstorm …

- How old is the tree?
- Are the flowers blooming?
- Are the petals falling?

Brainstorm …

- Focus on: Storyline.
  - Can you tell a story using this prompt?

Did you know?

We also make books to help with storytelling. With help on things like creating characters, world-building, magic systems, and more!

You can find more information on our website,
www.TCStudiosHQ.com.

#137 – Lavender. (M) (G) (C)

Brainstorm …

- Is it still on the bush?
- Is it in oil form?
- Is it being used as a remedy?

Brainstorm …

- Challenge: Color Palette.
    - Use a random color palette generator or ask a friend to pick 3-5 colors for you to use.

Did you know?

We also publish novels and comics that you can read!

You can find more information on our website,
www.TCStudiosHQ.com.

#138 – Aloe Vera. (W) (P) (AP)

Brainstorm …

- What kind?
- How big is it?
- Is it potted?
  - What kind of pot is it in?
  - What kind of soil is being used?
- Is it being used?
  - For a drink?
  - For a burn?

Brainstorm …

- Practice different types of shading techniques.
  - Hatching.
  - Cross-Hatching.
  - Stippling.
  - Scribbling.
  - Contour Lines.

Do you want to give us a prompt for next year's edition?

You can submit prompt ideas you have based on next year's chapter themes. Credit will be given if selected.

You can find more information on our website, www.TCStudiosHQ.com.

\#139 – Bamboo. (CP) (G) (M)

Brainstorm ...

- How tall is it?
- Is a panda eating it?
- Has it been used for furniture or an item?

Brainstorm ...

- Experiment: Comic Strip.
  - Try drawing this as a short comic strip.

Did you know?

We post daily writing & drawing prompts on our Social Medias for everyone to participate in.

Find us @PromptParty and use #PromptParty.

You can find more information on our website, www.TCStudiosHQ.com.

#140 – Peony. (W) (C) (I)

Brainstorm ...

- What color is it?
- Is it part of a bouquet?
- Is it in a jar/vase?
- Has it bloomed?

Brainstorm ...

- Experiment: Colored Lighting.
  - When/if you are applying lighting effects to this piece, try using a different color instead of just a lighter gradient of the lit area.

Drawing Exercise #28

Draw a bouquet of your favorite flowers.

#141 – Lily Pad. (P) (M) (AP)

Brainstorm …

- Where is it?
- Is the water around it clear?
- Is there a frog on it?
    - Is there something else on it?
    - Are there fish around it?

Brainstorm (Drawing) …

- Focus on: Background.
    - Tell the story with the use of the background and its environment. Think about the use and placement of specific items to help get the point across.

Did you know?

In addition to posting daily on Social Media, we have daily interactive posts on our YouTube channel, Podcast, and Blog.

You can find more information on our website, www.TCStudiosHQ.com.

#142 – Lily. (G) (I) (CP)

Brainstorm ...

- What color is it?
- Is it potted or natural?
- How many flowers are on the stem?

Brainstorm ...

- Challenge: Continuous line.
    - Try drawing this scene with one continuous line.
    - You can color the finished image.

Remember!

The listed genres/mediums and brainstorming boxes are **only suggestions!** We encourage you to do/use whatever you want.

#143 – Fern. (AP) (W) (P)

Brainstorm …

- What kind?
- How big is it?
- Is it potted?
- Is it hanging?
- Is it with other plants?

Brainstorm …

- Experiment: Bold Line Work.
  - When you've finished lining your work (if you're lining), try making some areas thicker than others.
    - It can be dramatically, or just a bit.
      - Take note of how it changes the tone of your work.

Be The First To Know.

Join our newsletter and be the first to know about new prompt books, novels, comics, giveaways, freebies, coupons, and anything else we've got going on!

Find our newsletter on our website, www.TCStudiosHQ.com.

#144 – Lilac. (M) (C) (AP)

Brainstorm …

- Is it in bunches?
- How tall is it?
- How old is the tree?
- How big is the bush?

Brainstorm …

- Challenge: Monochrome.
    - Try drawing this scene using only one gradient of color.

You can share your work with us on Facebook, Instagram & Twitter!

Tag us @PromptParty and use #PromptParty.

We'd love to see what you come up with!

#145 – Violet. (CP) (W) (G)

Brainstorm …

- Is it dark or light?
- What are the leaves like?
- Is it potted?
- Is it a part of a bouquet?

Brainstorm …

- Experiment: Comic Strip.
  - o Try drawing this as a short comic strip.

Drawing Exercise #29

Draw an animal grazing on some plants.

#146 – Tomato. (AP) (I) (CP)

<table><tr><td>

Brainstorm …

- What kind?
- Is it ripe?
- Is it still on the vine?
- What color is it?
- Is it being used to make something?
- Is it being thrown at someone?

</td><td>152</td></tr></table>

Brainstorm …

- Challenge: No Linework.
  - Try drawing this scene with no outlining – just dive right in with blocks of color!

Do you want your work published?

You can submit any work made using our prompts to our annual anthologies! Published submissions receive shared 25% royalties.

You can find more information on our website, www.TCStudiosHQ.com.

#147 – Green Onion. (P) (W) (C)

Brainstorm …

- Is it fresh or prechopped?
- What is it being used for?
- Where is it?
    - In the grocery store?
    - In a restaurant?
    - In someone's home?
    - In the ground?

Brainstorm …

- Practice: Hands.
    - Study up on some hand techniques and implement them in your drawing.
        - Maybe they're cutting the onion or cooking it.

Did you know?

A percentage of every anthology sold goes towards helping communities like yours. This includes donations to charities, funding of scholarships, creating of programs, and more!

You can find more information on our website, www.TCStudiosHQ.com.

#148 – Yucca. (G) (CP) (M)

Brainstorm …

- Is it potted?
  - Is it in the ground?
  - Where is it?
- Is it blooming?

Brainstorm …

- Experiment: Colored Lighting.
  - When/if you are applying lighting effects to this piece, try using a different color instead of just a lighter gradient of the lit area.

Did you know?

In addition to our annual prompt anthologies, every year we have <u>themed</u> anthologies that you can also submit to!

You can find more information on our website,
www.TCStudiosHQ.com.

\#149 – Spider Plant. (AP) (I) (W)

Brainstorm …

- How big is it?
- What shades of green are its leaves?
- Is it potted?
- Where is it?

Brainstorm …

- Challenge: No Linework.
    - Try drawing this scene with no outlining – just dive right in with blocks of color!

Looking for a challenge?

Try doing one of our prompts with your friend(s)! See if you can come up with something together.

\#150 – Philodendron. (C) (P) (G)

Brainstorm …

- What kind?
- What do the leaves look like?
- Is it potted?
- How big is it?
- Do the leaves hang?

Brainstorm …

- Focus on: Realism.
  - Try making the subject material for this prompt look as realistic as you can.

Drawing Exercise #30

Draw your ideal salad.

\#151 – Venus Fly Trap. (W) (M) (I)

Brainstorm ...

- Is it eating something?
- How big is it?
- Is it talking?
- Is it potted or in the ground?

Brainstorm ...

- Experiment: Comic Strip.
  - Try drawing this as a short comic strip.

Did you know?

We also make books to help with storytelling. With help on things like creating characters, world-building, magic systems, and more!

You can find more information on our website,
www.TCStudiosHQ.com.

\#152 – Calathea. (CP) (AP) (C)

Brainstorm …

- What kind?
- What color are the leaves?
- How big is it?
- Is it potted?
- Is it blooming?
- Where is it?

Brainstorm …

- Practice different types of shading techniques.
  - Hatching.
  - Cross-Hatching.
  - Stippling.
  - Scribbling.
  - Contour Lines.

Did you know?

We also publish novels and comics that you can read!

You can find more information on our website,
www.TCStudiosHQ.com.

Chapter Six: Technology.

#153 – Phone. (I) (M) (W)

Brainstorm …

- What kind/brand?
- Is it new or old?
- Is it a cellphone or landline?
- What apps are on the home screen?
- What battery percentage is it at?

Brainstorm …

- Life Study.
  - Go out and find this prompt to sketch.

Do you want to give us a prompt for next year's edition?

You can submit prompt ideas you have based on next year's chapter themes. Credit will be given if selected.

You can find more information on our website, www.TCStudiosHQ.com.

#154 – Radio. (W) (G) (M)

Brainstorm …

- What kind?
  - Box? Car?
- What station is on?
  - What kind of music is playing?
  - Is there a commercial on?
  - Is there static?
- Who is listening to it?

Brainstorm …

- Challenge: Secondary Colors.
  - Try drawing this scene using only secondary colors and their gradients.

Did you know?

We post daily writing & drawing prompts on our Social Medias for everyone to participate in.

Find us @PromptParty and use #PromptParty.

You can find more information on our website, www.TCStudiosHQ.com.

#155 – CD. (AP) (I) (G)

Brainstorm ...

- What kind?
  - Music?
  - Program?
  - DVD?
- What condition is it in?
- Where is it?

Brainstorm (Drawing) ...

- Practice: Texture.
  - Study texture techniques and implement them in your drawing.

Drawing Exercise #31

Draw 5 different types of phones.

\#156 – USB Drive. (W) (CP) (M)

<table>
<tr><td>

Brainstorm …

- What does it look like?
- What information is on it?
- Is it plugged in?
- Is someone using it?

</td></tr>
</table>

<table>
<tr><td>

Brainstorm …

- Challenge: Continuous line.
  - Try drawing this scene with one continuous line.
  - You can color the finished image.

</td></tr>
</table>

Did you know?

In addition to posting daily on Social Media, we have daily interactive posts on our YouTube channel, Podcast, and Blog.

You can find more information on our website, www.TCStudiosHQ.com.

\#157 – Television. (P) (AP) (G)

Brainstorm …

- What kind?
  - Box?
  - Flat screen?
- What's on?
  - The news?
  - Cartoons?
  - Video games?
  - Is it off?

Brainstorm …

- Challenge: Monochrome.
  - Try drawing this scene using only one gradient of color.

Remember!

The listed genres/mediums and brainstorming boxes are **only suggestions!** We encourage you to do/use whatever you want.

#158 – Computer. (I) (CP) (M)

Brainstorm …

- What kind?
  - Desktop?
  - Laptop?
  - Mac or Windows?
- What's on the screen?
  - Work?
  - Games?
  - Shows?
  - YouTube?

Brainstorm …

- Focus on: Background.
  - Tell the story with the use of the background and its environment. Think about the use and placement of specific items to help get the point across.

Be The First To Know.

Join our newsletter and be the first to know about new prompt books, novels, comics, giveaways, freebies, coupons, and anything else we've got going on!

Find our newsletter on our website, www.TCStudiosHQ.com.

164

\#159 – Car. (W) (P) (AP)

Brainstorm …

- What kind?
- What color is it?
- What condition is it in?
  - Has it been modified?
- Who's driving it?
- Where is it?

Brainstorm …

- Challenge: No references.
  - Put your muscle memory to the test and draw this scene without using any references.
    - Good luck!

You can share your work with us on Facebook, Instagram & Twitter!

Tag us @PromptParty and use #PromptParty.

We'd love to see what you come up with!

#160 – Assembly Line. (CP) (I) (C)

<table>
<tr><td>

Brainstorm ...

- How many people are working it?
- What's being made?
- How fast is it moving?
- What is the quality of the products?

</td></tr>
</table>

<table>
<tr><td>

Brainstorm ...

- Experiment: Comic Strip.
    - Try drawing this as a short comic strip.

</td></tr>
</table>

<table>
<tr><td>

Drawing Exercise #32

Draw 5 different types of game consoles/controllers.

</td></tr>
</table>

166

\#161 – iPod. (P) (M) (AP)

Brainstorm …

- What version?
- What is it playing?
- What condition is it in?
- What kind of headphones is it using?

Brainstorm …

- Practice: Hands.
    - Study up on some hand techniques and implement them in your drawing.
        - Maybe they're scrolling through their music or plugging in their charger.

Do you want your work published?

You can submit any work made using our prompts to our annual anthologies! Published submissions receive shared 25% royalties.

You can find more information on our website, www.TCStudiosHQ.com.

#162 – Air Conditioner. (CP) (G) (I)

Brainstorm …

- How hot is it?
- Is it too cold?
- Who is using it?
- Where is it?
- Is it working?

Brainstorm …

- Focus on: Background.
    - Tell the story with the use of the background and its environment. Think about the use and placement of specific items to help get the point across.

Did you know?

A percentage of every anthology sold goes towards helping communities like yours. This includes donations to charities, funding of scholarships, creating of programs, and more!

You can find more information on our website, www.TCStudiosHQ.com.

#163 – Hair Dryer. (W) (P) (AP)

Brainstorm ...

- Is it bulky or slim?
- Does it have any attachments?
- How hot does it get?
- What other kind of settings are there?
- Is it being used?
    - At home?
    - By a professional?

Brainstorm (Drawing) ...

- Challenge: Opposite Colors.
    - Pick a color and it's opposite (ex: red and green).
    - Try coloring this piece with only those two colors and their gradients.

Did you know?

In addition to our annual prompt anthologies, every year we have themed anthologies that you can also submit to!

You can find more information on our website, www.TCStudiosHQ.com.

\#164 – Plane. (CP) (M) (I)

Brainstorm ...

- How many passengers are there?
- Are there any pets on board?
- How full are the different class sections?
- Where is going?
- Where did it come from?
- Is it already flying or taking off?

Brainstorm ...

- Experiment: Colored Lighting.
  - When/if you are applying lighting effects to this piece, try using a different color instead of just a lighter gradient of the lit area.

Looking for a challenge?

Try doing one of our prompts with your friend(s)! See if you can come up with something together.

\#165 – Camera. (C) (AP) (I)

Brainstorm …

- What kind?
  - Phone?
  - Canon?
  - Polaroid?
- Is it being used?
  - By whom?

Brainstorm …

- Challenge: Color Palette.
  - Use a random color palette generator or ask a friend to pick 3-5 colors for you to use.

Drawing Exercise #33

Draw 5 different types of cameras.

171

\#166 – Headphones. (G) (P) (CP)

Brainstorm …

- What design do they have?
- Do they have any interesting features?
- Are they wired or Bluetooth?
- Are they being used?
- What color are they?
- What condition are they in?

Brainstorm …

- Experiment: Bold Line Work.
  - When you've finished lining your work (if you're lining), try making some areas thicker than others.
    - It can be dramatically, or just a bit.
      - Take note of how it changes the tone of your work.

Did you know?

We also make books to help with storytelling. With help on things like creating characters, world-building, magic systems, and more!

You can find more information on our website, www.TCStudiosHQ.com.

#167 – Robot. (M) (AP) (W)

Brainstorm ...

- Is it AI?
- How is it designed?
- Can it speak?
- What does it do?
- Who is using it?
- Is it owned?

Brainstorm ...

- Challenge: No Linework.
  - Try drawing this scene with no outlining – just dive right in with blocks of color!

Did you know?

We also publish novels and comics that you can read!

You can find more information on our website, www.TCStudiosHQ.com.

\#168 – Console Game. (P) (G) (I)

Brainstorm …   174

- How is the console designed?
- What kind of game is being played?
- Who is playing?
    o How many people?
        ▪ Are they enjoying themselves?
- What condition is the console in?

Brainstorm …

- Practice: Hands.
    o Study up on some hand techniques and implement them in your drawing.
        ▪ Maybe they're mashing buttons or putting in a game.

Do you want to give us a prompt for next year's edition?

You can submit prompt ideas you have based on next year's chapter themes. Credit will be given if selected.

You can find more information on our website, www.TCStudiosHQ.com.

#169 – VR Headset. (W) (C) (AP)

Brainstorm …

- What is the person seeing?
- What kind of game are they playing?
  - Are they playing a game at all?
- Are they enjoying the experience?
  - Are they scared?
  - Are they confused?
  - Are they in danger of knocking anything over?

Brainstorm …

- Practice: Anatomy.
  - Study proportions, positioning, and structure techniques and implement them in your drawing.

Did you know?

We post daily writing & drawing prompts on our Social Medias for everyone to participate in.

Find us @PromptParty and use #PromptParty.

You can find more information on our website, www.TCStudiosHQ.com.

#170 – Train. (I) (M) (P)

Brainstorm ...

- Is it old or modern?
- Where is it going?
  - Where is it coming from?
- How fast is it going?
- How many people are on it?
- What kind of scenery is around?

Brainstorm ...

- Practice different types of shading techniques.
  - Hatching.
  - Cross-Hatching.
  - Stippling.
  - Scribbling.
  - Contour Lines.

Drawing Exercise #34

Draw 5 different methods of transportation.

#171 – Internet. (AP) (G) (CP)

Brainstorm ...

- Is it fast or slow?
- What is it being used for?
- Is it connected?
  - Is it not working?

Brainstorm ...

- Challenge: Input.
  - Let someone tell you how you should set up your drawing and follow their instructions to the best of your ability.

Did you know?

In addition to posting daily on Social Media, we have daily interactive posts on our YouTube channel, Podcast, and Blog.

You can find more information on our website, www.TCStudiosHQ.com.

#172 – Hearing Aid. (P) (I) (M)

<table>
<tr><td>

Brainstorm …

- How is it designed?
- How effective is it?
- Who is using it?

</td></tr>
</table>

<table>
<tr><td>

Brainstorm …

- Challenge: Monochrome.
    - Try drawing this scene using only one gradient of color.

</td></tr>
</table>

Remember!

The listed genres/mediums and brainstorming boxes are **only suggestions!** We encourage you to do/use whatever you want.

178

#173 – X-Ray Machine. (W) (C) (I)

Brainstorm …

- What is being shown?
- Is there a problem?

Brainstorm …

- Challenge: Continuous line.
  - Try drawing this scene with one continuous line.
  - You can color the finished image.

Be The First To Know.

Join our newsletter and be the first to know about new prompt books, novels, comics, giveaways, freebies, coupons, and anything else we've got going on!

Find our newsletter on our website, www.TCStudiosHQ.com.

#174 – Vending Machine. (AP) (M) (G)

Brainstorm …

- What snacks or beverages are in the machine?
- What are the prices like?
- Is anyone using it?
- Is there a line?
- What condition is it in?

Brainstorm …

- Life Study.
  - Go out and find this prompt to sketch.

You can share your work with us on Facebook, Instagram & Twitter!

Tag us @PromptParty and use #PromptParty.

We'd love to see what you come up with!

\#175 – Remote. (CP) (P) (W)

Brainstorm …

- What is it for?
  - TV?
  - DVD player?
  - Stereo?
  - Lights?
- How is it designed?
- Does it use batteries?

Brainstorm …

- Challenge: Bird's Eye View.
  - Try drawing this piece with a bird's eye view.

Drawing Exercise #35

Draw 5 different types of cooking tools (i.e. blender, oven, microwave, etc.).

181

\#176 – GPS. (P) (M) (G)

Brainstorm …

- Where is it giving directions to?
- Are they accurate?
- Is the person lost?
- How is the GPS screen designed?

Brainstorm …

- Practice: Lighting.
    - Study color choice, gradients, and placement techniques of lighting and implement them in your drawing.

Do you want your work published?

You can submit any work made using our prompts to our annual anthologies! Published submissions receive shared 25% royalties.

You can find more information on our website, www.TCStudiosHQ.com.

\#177 – Speaker. (I) (C) (AP)

Brainstorm …

- How big is it?
- Is it being used?
- How loud is it?
  - Is it vibrating?
- Where is it?
- How many are there?

Brainstorm …

- Challenge: Life Reference.
  - See if you can take your own reference photos to use in your drawing.

Did you know?

A percentage of every anthology sold goes towards helping communities like yours. This includes donations to charities, funding of scholarships, creating of programs, and more!

You can find more information on our website, www.TCStudiosHQ.com.

#178 – Tracker. (W) (P) (G)

<table>
<tr><td>

Brainstorm ...

- What is being tracked?
  - An animal?
  - A person?
  - An object?
- Is it accurate?
- Where is the tracker placed?

</td></tr>
</table>

<table>
<tr><td>

Brainstorm ...

- Focus on: Storyline.
  - Can you tell a story using this prompt?

</td></tr>
</table>

Did you know?

In addition to our annual prompt anthologies, every year we have <u>themed</u> anthologies that you can also submit to!

You can find more information on our website, www.TCStudiosHQ.com.

\#179 – Stove/Oven. (CP) (M) (I)

Brainstorm …

- Is it old or modern?
- What kind?
  - Wood?
  - Gas?
  - Electric?
- Is it being used?
  - Who is using it?
  - What is it being used for?

Brainstorm …

- Challenge: Secondary Colors.
  - Try drawing this scene using only secondary colors and their gradients.

Looking for a challenge?

Try doing one of our prompts with your friend(s)! See if you can come up with something together.

185

\#180 – Refrigerator. (G) (AP) (P)

<table>
<tr><td>

Brainstorm …

- How big is it?
- Is a single or double door?
- Is it empty or full?
- Is it "smart"?
- Are the doors open or closed?

</td></tr>
</table>

<table>
<tr><td>

Brainstorm …

- Experiment: Colored Lighting.
  - When/if you are applying lighting effects to this piece, try using a different color instead of just a lighter gradient of the lit area.

</td></tr>
</table>

<table>
<tr><td>

Drawing Exercise #36

Draw 5 different types of computers.

</td></tr>
</table>

#181 – Credit/Debit Card. (W) (I) (C)

Brainstorm ...

- What color is it?
- Does it have a chip?
- How many are there?
- Where are they kept?
- Are they maxed out or cut up?
- Is there a design on it?

Brainstorm ...

- Experiment: Bold Line Work.
  - When you've finished lining your work (if you're lining), try making some areas thicker than others.
    - It can be dramatically, or just a bit.
      - Take note of how it changes the tone of your work.

Did you know?

We also make books to help with storytelling. With help on things like creating characters, world-building, magic systems, and more!

You can find more information on our website,
www.TCStudiosHQ.com.

\#182 – Surgical Implant. (M) (G) (CP)

Brainstorm ...

- Where has it been placed?
- How does it work?
- What does it do?
- How does the patient feel about it?
- Was the surgery successful?
- What is their life like with it?

Brainstorm ...

- Practice different types of shading techniques.
    - Hatching.
    - Cross-Hatching.
    - Stippling.
    - Scribbling.
    - Contour Lines.

Did you know?

We also publish novels and comics that you can read!

You can find more information on our website,
www.TCStudiosHQ.com.

\#183 – Robotic Limb. (P) (W) (M)

Brainstorm ...

- Which limb?
- How is it designed?
- How functional is it?
- Is it steampunk? Modern?

Brainstorm ...

- Experiment: Exaggerated Proportions/Features.
  - Get a little cartoony.
  - How might exaggerating certain features help the imagery?

Do you want to give us a prompt for next year's edition?

You can submit prompt ideas you have based on next year's chapter themes. Credit will be given if selected.

You can find more information on our website, www.TCStudiosHQ.com.

Chapter Seven: Emotion.

#184 – Awed. (I) (C) (AP)

<table>
<tr><td>

Brainstorm ...

- About what?
- How does this affect their facial expression?
- How does this affect their body language?
- Is anyone else involved?

</td></tr>
</table>

<table>
<tr><td>

Brainstorm (Drawing) ...

- Challenge: Opposite Colors.
    - Pick a color and it's opposite (ex: red and green).
    - Try coloring this piece with only those two colors and their gradients.

</td></tr>
</table>

Did you know?

We post daily writing & drawing prompts on our Social Medias for everyone to participate in.

Find us @PromptParty and use #PromptParty.

You can find more information on our website, www.TCStudiosHQ.com.

#185 – Enraged. (CP) (G) (P)

Brainstorm …

- About what?
- How does this affect their facial expression?
- How does this affect their body language?
- Is anyone else involved?

Brainstorm …

- Focus on: Body Language.
  - How can you position the body to emphasize this prompt?

Drawing Exercise #37

Draw 5 different expressions of joy.

191

\#186 – Confused. (M) (I) (C)

Brainstorm ...

- About what?
- How does this affect their facial expression?
- How does this affect their body language?
- Is anyone else involved?

Brainstorm ...

- Challenge: No references.
    - Put your muscle memory to the test and draw this scene without using any references.
        - Good luck!

Did you know?

In addition to posting daily on Social Media, we have daily interactive posts on our YouTube channel, Podcast, and Blog.

You can find more information on our website,
www.TCStudiosHQ.com.

\#187 – Desperate. (M) (AP) (W)

Brainstorm …

- About what?
- How does this affect their facial expression?
- How does this affect their body language?
- Is anyone else involved?

Brainstorm …

- Challenge: Self-Portrait.
    - Draw yourself into this scene.

Remember!

The listed genres/mediums and brainstorming boxes are **only suggestions!** We encourage you to do/use whatever you want.

\#188 – Joyful. (P) (CP) (I)

Brainstorm ...

- About what?
- How does this affect their facial expression?
- How does this affect their body language?
- Is anyone else involved?

Brainstorm ...

- Practice: Skin Tones.
  - Study skin tone palettes and techniques and implement them in your drawing.

Be The First To Know.

Join our newsletter and be the first to know about new prompt books, novels, comics, giveaways, freebies, coupons, and anything else we've got going on!

Find our newsletter on our website, www.TCStudiosHQ.com.

#189 – Excited. (M) (G) (AP)

Brainstorm …

- About what?
- How does this affect their facial expression?
- How does this affect their body language?
- Is anyone else involved?

Brainstorm …

- Challenge: No Linework.
    - Try drawing this scene with no outlining – just dive right in with blocks of color!

You can share your work with us on Facebook, Instagram & Twitter!

Tag us @PromptParty and use #PromptParty.

We'd love to see what you come up with!

#190 – Fearful. (I) (W) (CP)

Brainstorm …

- About what?
- How does this affect their facial expression?
- How does this affect their body language?
- Is anyone else involved?

Brainstorm …

- Challenge: Color Palette.
  - Use a random color palette generator or ask a friend to pick 3-5 colors for you to use.

Drawing Exercise #38

Draw 5 different expressions of sorrow.

\#191 – Anxious. (C) (M) (P)

Brainstorm ...

- About what?
- How does this affect their facial expression?
- How does this affect their body language?
- Is anyone else involved?

Brainstorm ...

- Practice: Hands.
  - Study up on some hand techniques and implement them in your drawing.
    - Maybe they're rigging their hands or biting their nails.

Do you want your work published?

You can submit any work made using our prompts to our annual anthologies! Published submissions receive shared 25% royalties.

You can find more information on our website, www.TCStudiosHQ.com.

\#192 – Sad. (AP) (W) (CP)

Brainstorm ...

- About what?
- How does this affect their facial expression?
- How does this affect their body language?
- Is anyone else involved?

Brainstorm ...

- Practice: Lighting.
  - Study color choice, gradients, and placement techniques of lighting and implement them in your drawing.

Did you know?

A percentage of every anthology sold goes towards helping communities like yours. This includes donations to charities, funding of scholarships, creating of programs, and more!

You can find more information on our website, www.TCStudiosHQ.com.

\#193 – Hyper. (G) (P) (I)

Brainstorm ...

- About what?
- How does this affect their facial expression?
- How does this affect their body language?
- Is anyone else involved?

Brainstorm (Drawing) ...

- Practice: Texture.
    - Study texture techniques and implement them in your drawing.

Did you know?

In addition to our annual prompt anthologies, every year we have
themed anthologies that you can also submit to!

You can find more information on our website,
www.TCStudiosHQ.com.

#194 – Love. (M) (AP) (I)

Brainstorm …

- About/with what/who?
- How does this affect their facial expression?
- How does this affect their body language?
- Is anyone else involved?

Brainstorm …

- Experiment: Comic Strip.
  - Try drawing this as a short comic strip.

Looking for a challenge?

Try doing one of our prompts with your friend(s)! See if you can
come up with something together.

#195 – Boredom. (P) (G) (CP)

Brainstorm ...

- Why?
- How does this affect their facial expression?
- How does this affect their body language?
- Is anyone else involved?

Brainstorm ...

- Practice: Hair.
  - Study the flow and lighting dimensions of hair and implement the techniques into your drawing.

Drawing Exercise #39

Draw 5 different expressions of love.

\#196 – Anticipation. (W) (C) (I)

Brainstorm …

- About what?
- How does this affect their facial expression?
- How does this affect their body language?
- Is anyone else involved?

Brainstorm …

- Challenge: Continuous line.
    - o Try drawing this scene with one continuous line.
    - o You can color the finished image.

Did you know?

We also make books to help with storytelling. With help on things like creating characters, world-building, magic systems, and more!

You can find more information on our website, www.TCStudiosHQ.com.

\#197 – Depressed. (M) (AP) (G)

Brainstorm …

- About what? Why?
- How does this affect their facial expression?
- How does this affect their body language?
- Is anyone else involved?

Brainstorm …

- Experiment: Colored Lighting.
    - When/if you are applying lighting effects to this piece, try using a different color instead of just a lighter gradient of the lit area.

Did you know?

We also publish novels and comics that you can read!

You can find more information on our website, www.TCStudiosHQ.com.

#198 – Sleepy. (CP) (I) (P)

Brainstorm …

- Why? When?
- How does this affect their facial expression?
- How does this affect their body language?
- Is anyone else involved?

Brainstorm …

- Practice: Skin Tones.
  - Study skin tone palettes and techniques and implement them in your drawing.

Do you want to give us a prompt for next year's edition?

You can submit prompt ideas you have based on next year's chapter themes. Credit will be given if selected.

You can find more information on our website, www.TCStudiosHQ.com.

#199 – Hopeful. (W) (M) (AP)

Brainstorm …

- About what?
- How does this affect their facial expression?
- How does this affect their body language?
- Is anyone else involved?

Brainstorm …

- Practice: Anatomy.
  - Study proportions, positioning, and structure techniques and implement them in your drawing.

Did you know?

We post daily writing & drawing prompts on our Social Medias for everyone to participate in.

Find us @PromptParty and use #PromptParty.

You can find more information on our website, www.TCStudiosHQ.com.

#200 – Resentful. (G) (W) (CP)

Brainstorm ...

- About what?
- How does this affect their facial expression?
- How does this affect their body language?
- Is anyone else involved?

Brainstorm ...

- Challenge: Monochrome.
  - Try drawing this scene using only one gradient of color.

Drawing Exercise #40

Draw 5 different expressions of anger.

206

#201 – Guilty. (P) (M) (AP)

Brainstorm …

- About what?
- How does this affect their facial expression?
- How does this affect their body language?
- Is anyone else involved?

Brainstorm …

- Experiment: Bold Line Work.
  - When you've finished lining your work (if you're lining), try making some areas thicker than others.
    - It can be dramatically, or just a bit.
      - Take note of how it changes the tone of your work.

Did you know?

In addition to posting daily on Social Media, we have daily interactive posts on our YouTube channel, Podcast, and Blog.

You can find more information on our website, www.TCStudiosHQ.com.

\#202 – Invincible. (I) (C) (W)

Brainstorm ...

- How? Why?
- How does this affect their facial expression?
- How does this affect their body language?
- Is anyone else involved?

Brainstorm ...

- Focus on: Body Language.
    - How can you position the body to emphasize this prompt?

Remember!

The listed genres/mediums and brainstorming boxes are **only suggestions!** We encourage you to do/use whatever you want.

\#203 – Jealous. (CP) (M) (G)

Brainstorm ...

- About what?
- How does this affect their facial expression?
- How does this affect their body language?
- Is anyone else involved?

Brainstorm ...

- Focus on: Background.
  - Tell the story with the use of the background and its environment. Think about the use and placement of specific items to help get the point across.

Be The First To Know.

Join our newsletter and be the first to know about new prompt books, novels, comics, giveaways, freebies, coupons, and anything else we've got going on!

Find our newsletter on our website, www.TCStudiosHQ.com.

#204 – Lonely. (P) (C) (AP)

Brainstorm ...

- Why?
- How does this affect their facial expression?
- How does this affect their body language?
- Is anyone else involved?

Brainstorm ...

- Challenge: Input.
  - Let someone tell you how you should set up your drawing and follow their instructions to the best of your ability.

You can share your work with us on Facebook, Instagram & Twitter!

Tag us @PromptParty and use #PromptParty.

We'd love to see what you come up with!

#205 – Annoyed. (W) (I) (CP)

Brainstorm ...

- About what?
- How does this affect their facial expression?
- How does this affect their body language?
- Is anyone else involved?

Brainstorm ...

- Challenge: Secondary Colors.
    - Try drawing this scene using only secondary colors and their gradients.

Drawing Exercise #41

Draw 5 different expressions of anxiety.

\#206 – Stressed. (P) (M) (AP)

Brainstorm …

- About what?
- How does this affect their facial expression?
- How does this affect their body language?
- Is anyone else involved?

Brainstorm …

- Practice different types of shading techniques.
  - Hatching.
  - Cross-Hatching.
  - Stippling.
  - Scribbling.
  - Contour Lines.

Do you want your work published?

You can submit any work made using our prompts to our annual anthologies! Published submissions receive shared 25% royalties.

You can find more information on our website,
www.TCStudiosHQ.com.

#207 – Protective. (G) (C) (I)

<table>
<tr><td>

Brainstorm …

- About what?
- How does this affect their facial expression?
- How does this affect their body language?
- Is anyone else involved?

</td></tr>
</table>

<table>
<tr><td>

Brainstorm …

- Experiment: Exaggerated Proportions/Features.
  - Get a little cartoony.
  - How might exaggerating certain features help the imagery?

</td></tr>
</table>

Did you know?

A percentage of every anthology sold goes towards helping communities like yours. This includes donations to charities, funding of scholarships, creating of programs, and more!

You can find more information on our website, www.TCStudiosHQ.com.

\#208 – Curious. (W) (P) (CP)

Brainstorm ...

- About what?
- How does this affect their facial expression?
- How does this affect their body language?
- Is anyone else involved?

Brainstorm ...

- Challenge: Continuous line.
  - Try drawing this scene with one continuous line.
  - You can color the finished image.

Did you know?

In addition to our annual prompt anthologies, every year we have <u>themed</u> anthologies that you can also submit to!

You can find more information on our website,
www.TCStudiosHQ.com.

#209 – Cautious. (M) (G) (AP)

Brainstorm ...

- About what?
- How does this affect their facial expression?
- How does this affect their body language?
- Is anyone else involved?

Brainstorm ...

- Challenge: Bird's Eye View.
    - Try drawing this piece with a bird's eye view.

Looking for a challenge?

Try doing one of our prompts with your friend(s)! See if you can
come up with something together.

#210 – Skeptical. (I) (P) (W)

Brainstorm …

- About what?
- How does this affect their facial expression?
- How does this affect their body language?
- Is anyone else involved?

Brainstorm (Drawing) …

- Challenge: Opposite Colors.
    - Pick a color and it's opposite (ex: red and green).
    - Try coloring this piece with only those two colors and their gradients.

Drawing Exercise #42

Draw 5 different expressions of surprise.

#211 – Disgusted. (CP) (G) (C)

Brainstorm ...

- About what?
- How does this affect their facial expression?
- How does this affect their body language?
- Is anyone else involved?

Brainstorm ...

- Focus on: Storyline.
    - Can you tell a story using this prompt?

Did you know?

We also make books to help with storytelling. With help on things like creating characters, world-building, magic systems, and more!

You can find more information on our website, www.TCStudiosHQ.com.

\#212 – Judgmental. (M) (C) (G)

Brainstorm ...

- About what?
- How does this affect their facial expression?
- How does this affect their body language?
- Is anyone else involved?

Brainstorm ...

- Challenge: No Linework.
    - Try drawing this scene with no outlining – just dive right in with blocks of color!

Did you know?

We also publish novels and comics that you can read!

You can find more information on our website, www.TCStudiosHQ.com.

\#213 – Nostalgic. (P) (AP) (W)

Brainstorm …

- About what?
- How does this affect their facial expression?
- How does this affect their body language?
- Is anyone else involved?

Brainstorm …

- Challenge: No Linework.
    - Try drawing this scene with no outlining – just dive right in with blocks of color!

Do you want to give us a prompt for next year's edition?

You can submit prompt ideas you have based on next year's chapter themes. Credit will be given if selected.

You can find more information on our website, www.TCStudiosHQ.com.

#214 – Awkward. (CP) (M) (I)

Brainstorm …

- About what?
- How does this affect their facial expression?
- How does this affect their body language?
- Is anyone else involved?

Brainstorm …

- Challenge: No references.
  - o Put your muscle memory to the test and draw this scene without using any references.
    - Good luck!

Did you know?

We post daily writing & drawing prompts on our Social Medias for everyone to participate in.

Find us @PromptParty and use #PromptParty.

You can find more information on our website, www.TCStudiosHQ.com.

Chapter Eight: Magic.

#215 – Potion. (P) (W) (C)

Brainstorm …

- What kind?
    - o   Is it harmful or helpful?
    - o   What ingredients are in it?
    - o   What color is it?
    - o   What kind of bottle is it in?

Brainstorm …

- Focus on: Realism.
    - o   Try making the subject material for this prompt look as realistic as you can.

Drawing Exercise #43

Draw a collection of scrolls.

#216 – Spell. (AP) (M) (G)

Brainstorm …

- What kind?
  - Is it harmful or helpful?
- Is it written down?
- Is it being said?
- Who is casting it?

Brainstorm …

- Experiment: Comic Strip.
  - Try drawing this as a short comic strip.

Did you know?

In addition to posting daily on Social Media, we have daily interactive posts on our YouTube channel, Podcast, and Blog.

You can find more information on our website,
www.TCStudiosHQ.com.

\#217 – Wizard. (P) (I) (CP)

Brainstorm ...

- What kind?
  - Good or bad?
- Do they have a specialization?
- What kind of clothing do they wear?
- Do they have a hat?
- What are they doing?

Brainstorm ...

- Challenge: Self-Portrait.
  - Draw yourself into this scene.

Remember!

The listed genres/mediums and brainstorming boxes are **only suggestions!** We encourage you to do/use whatever you want.

\#218 – Witch. (M) (AP) (W)

Brainstorm …

- What kind?
  - Good or bad?
- Do they have a specialization?
- What kind of clothing do they wear?
- Do they have a hat?
- What are they doing?

Brainstorm …

- Practice: Skin Tones.
  - Study skin tone palettes and techniques and implement them in your drawing.

Be The First To Know.

Join our newsletter and be the first to know about new prompt books, novels, comics, giveaways, freebies, coupons, and anything else we've got going on!

Find our newsletter on our website, www.TCStudiosHQ.com.

#219 – Curse. (G) (I) (M)

Brainstorm ...

- On whom/what?
- Why?
- What does it do?
- Cast by whom?

Brainstorm ...

- Challenge: Monochrome.
  - Try drawing this scene using only one gradient of color.

You can share your work with us on Facebook, Instagram & Twitter!

Tag us @PromptParty and use #PromptParty.

We'd love to see what you come up with!

#220 – Brewing Pot. (CP) (AP) (P)

Brainstorm ...

- What's being made?
  - By whom?
- What ingredients are being used?
- What does the environment around this scene look like?

Brainstorm ...

- Experiment: Colored Lighting.
  - When/if you are applying lighting effects to this piece, try using a different color instead of just a lighter gradient of the lit area.

Drawing Exercise #44

Draw a collection of potions.

#221 – Magician. (W) (I) (C)

Brainstorm ...

- What kind of tricks do they do?
- Where are they performing?
  - On the street?
  - On a stage?
  - At a party?
- How are they dressed?

Brainstorm (Drawing) ...

- Focus on: Background.
  - Tell the story with the use of the background and its environment. Think about the use and placement of specific items to help get the point across.

Do you want your work published?

You can submit any work made using our prompts to our annual anthologies! Published submissions receive shared 25% royalties.

You can find more information on our website,
www.TCStudiosHQ.com.

#222 – Magic Trick. (G) (AP) (M)

Brainstorm …

- What does it do?
- What does it entail?
- Who is performing it?
- Is it just a trick or real magic?
- What is the reaction to it?

Brainstorm …

- Practice: Hands.
  - Study up on some hand techniques and implement them in your drawing.
    - Maybe they're spreading out a deck of cards or pulling a rabbit out of a hat.

Did you know?

A percentage of every anthology sold goes towards helping communities like yours. This includes donations to charities, funding of scholarships, creating of programs, and more!

You can find more information on our website, www.TCStudiosHQ.com.

#223 – Potion Ingredients. (P) (CP) (W)

Brainstorm ...

- What are they?
- Where are they?
    - Where do you get them?
- Are they being used?
    - To make what?

Brainstorm ...

- Experiment: Bold Line Work.
    - When you've finished lining your work (if you're lining), try making some areas thicker than others.
        - It can be dramatically, or just a bit.
            - Take note of how it changes the tone of your work.

Did you know?

In addition to our annual prompt anthologies, every year we have <u>themed</u> anthologies that you can also submit to!

You can find more information on our website,
www.TCStudiosHQ.com.

\#224 – Scroll. (I) (M) (AP)

Brainstorm ...

- What does it say?
- How is it written?
- Is someone reading it?
    - Who?
    - Why?
- What condition is it in?

Brainstorm ...

- Challenge: No references.
    - Put your muscle memory to the test and draw this scene without using any references.
        - Good luck!

Looking for a challenge?

Try doing one of our prompts with your friend(s)! See if you can come up with something together.

#225 – Magic School. (G) (P) (C)

Brainstorm ...

- What kinds of things does it teach?
- What does it look like?
- How many students are there?
- What are the teachers like?
- What are the students like?

Brainstorm ...

- Practice different types of shading techniques.
    - Hatching.
    - Cross-Hatching.
    - Stippling.
    - Scribbling.
    - Contour Lines.

Drawing Exercise #45

Draw a collection of magic broom sticks.

#226 – Wand. (AP) (CP) (W)

Brainstorm ...   232

- What kind?
- What is it made of?
- Is there an engraving?
- Is it being used?
- Are there any designs on it?

Brainstorm ...

- Challenge: Continuous line.
    - Try drawing this scene with one continuous line.
    - You can color the finished image.

Did you know?

We also make books to help with storytelling. With help on things like creating characters, world-building, magic systems, and more!

You can find more information on our website,
www.TCStudiosHQ.com.

#227 – Witch's Hat. (P) (M) (I)

Brainstorm …

- How big is it?
- What color is it?
- What condition is it in?
- Is it being worn?
- Are there any designs/features on it?

Brainstorm (Drawing) …

- Practice: Texture.
    - Study texture techniques and implement them in your drawing.

Did you know?

We also publish novels and comics that you can read!

You can find more information on our website,
www.TCStudiosHQ.com.

#228 – Water Witch/Wizard. (G) (CP) (C)

Brainstorm …

- Good or bad?
- How do they use their element?
- How does it affect their style?
    - How do they dress?
    - Do they have an aesthetic?
- What kinds of spells and potions do they use?
- Where might they live?

Brainstorm …

- Challenge: No Linework.
    - Try drawing this scene with no outlining – just dive right in with blocks of color!

Do you want to give us a prompt for next year's edition?

You can submit prompt ideas you have based on next year's chapter themes. Credit will be given if selected.

You can find more information on our website, www.TCStudiosHQ.com.

#229 – Fire Witch/Wizard. (W) (I) (M)

Brainstorm …

- Good or bad?
- How do they use their element?
- How does it affect their style?
    - How do they dress?
    - Do they have an aesthetic?
- What kinds of spells and potions do they use?
- Where might they live?

Brainstorm …

- Challenge: Color Palette.
    - Use a random color palette generator or ask a friend to pick 3-5 colors for you to use.

Did you know?

We post daily writing & drawing prompts on our Social Medias for everyone to participate in.

Find us @PromptParty and use #PromptParty.

You can find more information on our website, www.TCStudiosHQ.com.

#230 – Earth Witch/Wizard. (P) (AP) (G)

Brainstorm …

- Good or bad?
- How do they use their element?
- How does it affect their style?
  - How do they dress?
  - Do they have an aesthetic?
- What kinds of spells and potions do they use?
- Where might they live?

Brainstorm …

- Practice: Hair.
  - Study the flow and lighting of hair and implement the techniques into your drawing.

Drawing Exercise #46

Draw a collection of magic wands.

\#231 – Air Witch/Wizard. (C) (CP) (I)

Brainstorm …

- Good or bad?
- How do they use their element?
- How does it affect their style?
    - How do they dress?
    - Do they have an aesthetic?
- What kinds of spells and potions do they use?
- Where might they live?

Brainstorm …

- Practice: Skin Tones.
    - Study skin tone palettes and techniques and implement them in your drawing.

Did you know?

In addition to posting daily on Social Media, we have daily interactive posts on our YouTube channel, Podcast, and Blog.

You can find more information on our website, www.TCStudiosHQ.com.

#232 – Necromancer. (G) (W) (AP)

Brainstorm ...

- Good or bad?
- How do they use their element?
- How does it affect their style?
    - How do they dress?
    - Do they have an aesthetic?
- What kinds of spells and potions do they use?
- Where might they live?

Brainstorm ...

- Experiment: Colored Lighting.
    - When/if you are applying lighting effects to this piece, try using a different color instead of just a lighter gradient of the lit area.

Remember!

The listed genres/mediums and brainstorming boxes are **only suggestions!** We encourage you to do/use whatever you want.

#233 – Sorcerer. (P) (M) (I)

Brainstorm …

- What kind of magic do they use?
- Are they good or bad?
- How are they dressed?
- Are they old fashioned or modern?
- Are they an expert or amateur?

Brainstorm …

- Practice: Hands.
  - Study up on some hand techniques and implement them in your drawing.
    - Maybe they're casting a spell, or holding a scroll, or waving their wand.

Be The First To Know.

Join our newsletter and be the first to know about new prompt books, novels, comics, giveaways, freebies, coupons, and anything else we've got going on!

Find our newsletter on our website, www.TCStudiosHQ.com.

#234 – Magic Creature. (C) (W) (G)

Brainstorm …

- Where does it live?
- What color is it?
- Does it have wings?
- Does it have fins?
- Can it breathe underwater?
- Does it have feathers? Scales?
- How many limbs does it have?
- How many eyes? Mouths? Etc.?

Brainstorm …

- Challenge: Input.
  - Let someone tell you how you should set up your drawing and follow their instructions to the best of your ability.

You can share your work with us on Facebook, Instagram & Twitter!

Tag us @PromptParty and use #PromptParty.

We'd love to see what you come up with!

#235 – Spell Book. (AP) (G) (P)

Brainstorm ...

- What kind of spells are in it?
- What condition is it in?
- Where is it?
- Is someone reading it?
- Is it locked away?

Brainstorm ...

- Challenge: Secondary Colors.
    - Try drawing this scene using only secondary colors and their gradients.

Drawing Exercise #47

Draw a collection of witch/wizard hats.

#236 – Disappearing. (I) (M) (W)

Brainstorm ...

- What's disappearing?
- Why?
- What is the reaction to it?
- Are they showing up somewhere else?
- Is it happening slowly or all at once?

Brainstorm ...

- Challenge: Bird's Eye View.
    - Try drawing this piece with a bird's eye view.

Do you want your work published?

You can submit any work made using our prompts to our annual anthologies! Published submissions receive shared 25% royalties.

You can find more information on our website, www.TCStudiosHQ.com.

#237 – Broom Stick. (CP) (C) (AP)

Brainstorm ...

- What kind of wood is it?
  - Is it made of something else?
    - Metal?
    - Bone?
- What condition is it in?
- Is it being used?
  - How so?
  - By whom/what?

Brainstorm ...

- Challenge: No references.
  - Put your muscle memory to the test and draw this scene without using any references.
    - Good luck!

Did you know?

A percentage of every anthology sold goes towards helping communities like yours. This includes donations to charities, funding of scholarships, creating of programs, and more!

You can find more information on our website, www.TCStudiosHQ.com.

\#238 – Magical Girl. (G) (W) (I)

Brainstorm …

- What kind of magic do they do?
- Are they young or old?
- What are they wearing?
- Are they good or bad?
- How do they use their magic?
- Are they good or bad at it?

Brainstorm …

- Practice: Anatomy.
  - Study proportions, positioning, and structure techniques and implement them in your drawing.

Did you know?

In addition to our annual prompt anthologies, every year we have <u>themed</u> anthologies that you can also submit to!

You can find more information on our website, www.TCStudiosHQ.com.

#239 – Magical Boy. (CP) (W) (P)

Brainstorm ...

- What kind of magic do they do?
- Are they young or old?
- What are they wearing?
- Are they good or bad?
- How do they use their magic?
- Are they good or bad at it?

Brainstorm (Drawing) ...

- Challenge: Opposite Colors.
    - Pick a color and it's opposite (ex: red and green).
    - Try coloring this piece with only those two colors and their gradients.

Looking for a challenge?

Try doing one of our prompts with your friend(s)! See if you can come up with something together.

#240 – Bottomless Bag. (I) (AP) (G)

> ***Brainstorm …***
>
> - What's in it?
>   - Is anything living?
>   - How big are the items?
>   - What kind of uses do they have?
> - Who's using it?

> ***Brainstorm …***
>
> - Experiment: Exaggerated Proportions/Features.
>   - Get a little cartoony.
>   - How might exaggerating certain features help the imagery?

Drawing Exercise #48

Draw a group of magical creatures.

\#241 – Witch/Wizard's Home. (W) (I) (P)

<table>
<tr><td>

__Brainstorm ...__

- Where is it?
- How big/small is it?
- What kinds of things are inside?
- Is it tidy or messy?
- Is any magic happening?
- How is it decorated?
- What's the outside like?
    - How is that kept/decorated?

</td></tr>
</table>

<table>
<tr><td>

__Brainstorm ...__

- Focus on: Storyline.
    - Can you tell a story using this prompt?

</td></tr>
</table>

Did you know?

We also make books to help with storytelling. With help on things like creating characters, world-building, magic systems, and more!

You can find more information on our website,
www.TCStudiosHQ.com.

#242 – Potion Shop. (G) (AP) (M)

Brainstorm ...

- Is it big or small?
- Are there a lot of people inside?
- What kinds of potions do they have?
- How are they organized?
- Are there any samples?
- Are any being made?
- Are any being purchased?
- Are any being used?

Brainstorm ...

- Practice: Lighting.
    - Study color choice, gradients, and placement techniques of lighting and implement them in your drawing.

Did you know?

We also publish novels and comics that you can read!

You can find more information on our website,
www.TCStudiosHQ.com.

#243 – Scroll Shop. (C) (CP) (P)

Brainstorm …

- Is it big or small?
- Are there a lot of people inside?
- What kinds of scrolls do they have?
- How are they organized?
- Are any being made?
- Are any being purchased?
- Are any being used?

Brainstorm (Drawing) …

- Focus on: Background.
  - Tell the story with the use of the background and its environment. Think about the use and placement of specific items to help get the point across.

Do you want to give us a prompt for next year's edition?

You can submit prompt ideas you have based on next year's chapter themes. Credit will be given if selected.

You can find more information on our website, www.TCStudiosHQ.com.

\#244 – Magical Professor. (W) (M) (G)

Brainstorm …

- What do they teach?
- Where do they teach?
- How are they dressed?
- How many students do they have?

Brainstorm …

- Challenge: Continuous line.
    - Try drawing this scene with one continuous line.
    - You can color the finished image.

Did you know?

We post daily writing & drawing prompts on our Social Medias for everyone to participate in.

Find us @PromptParty and use #PromptParty.

You can find more information on our website, www.TCStudiosHQ.com.

Chapter Nine: Clothes.

#245 – Cardigan. (AP) (I) (P)

Brainstorm …

- What material is it?
- What color is it?
- Does it have any patterns?
- How is it being worn?
- Is it hanging up/folded/tossed about?
- What condition is it in?
- Are there any features/interesting designs?

Brainstorm …

- Challenge: Life Reference.
  - See if you can take your own reference photos to use in your drawing.

Drawing Exercise #49

Draw an outfit with a goth aesthetic.

\#246 – Jeans. (M) (CP) (G)

Brainstorm ...

- What color is it?
- Does it have any patterns?
- How is it being worn?
- Is it hanging up/folded/tossed about?
- What condition is it in?
- Are there any features/interesting designs?

Brainstorm ...

- Challenge: Monochrome.
  - Try drawing this scene using only one gradient of color.

Did you know?

In addition to posting daily on Social Media, we have daily interactive posts on our YouTube channel, Podcast, and Blog.

You can find more information on our website, www.TCStudiosHQ.com.

#247 – T-Shirt. (W) (C) (AP)

Brainstorm ...

- What material is it?
- What color is it?
- Does it have any patterns?
- How is it being worn?
- Is it hanging up/folded/tossed about?
- What condition is it in?
- Are there any features/interesting designs?

Brainstorm ...

- Focus on: Background.
  - Tell the story with the use of the background and its environment. Think about the use and placement of specific items to help get the point across.

Remember!

The listed genres/mediums and brainstorming boxes are **only suggestions!** We encourage you to do/use whatever you want.

#248 – Shorts. (G) (I) (CP)

Brainstorm …

- What material is it?
- What color is it?
- Does it have any patterns?
- How is it being worn?
- Is it hanging up/folded/tossed about?
- What condition is it in?
- Are there any features/interesting designs?

Brainstorm …

- Focus on: Realism.
  - Try making the subject material for this prompt look as realistic as you can.

Be The First To Know.

Join our newsletter and be the first to know about new prompt books, novels, comics, giveaways, freebies, coupons, and anything else we've got going on!

Find our newsletter on our website, www.TCStudiosHQ.com.

#249 – Pajamas. (M) (W) (I)

Brainstorm …

- What material is it?
- What color is it?
- Does it have any patterns?
- How is it being worn?
- Is it hanging up/folded/tossed about?
- What condition is it in?
- Are there any features/interesting designs?

Brainstorm …

- Challenge: Color Palette.
  - Use a random color palette generator or ask a friend to pick 3-5 colors for you to use.

You can share your work with us on Facebook, Instagram & Twitter!

Tag us @PromptParty and use #PromptParty.

We'd love to see what you come up with!

#250 – Romper. (P) (AP) (G)

Brainstorm …   256

- What material is it?
- What color is it?
- Does it have any patterns?
- How is it being worn?
- Is it hanging up/folded/tossed about?
- What condition is it in?
- Are there any features/interesting designs?

Brainstorm …

- Challenge: Opposite Colors.
  - Pick a color and it's opposite (ex: red and green).
  - Try coloring this piece with only those two colors and their gradients.

Drawing Exercise #50

Draw an outfit with a retro aesthetic.

#251 – Leather Jacket. (W) (CP) (C)

Brainstorm …

- What color is it?
- Does it have any patterns?
- How is it being worn?
- Is it hanging up/folded/tossed about?
- What condition is it in?
- Are there any features/interesting designs?

Brainstorm …

- Practice different types of shading techniques.
  - Hatching.
  - Cross-Hatching.
  - Stippling.
  - Scribbling.
  - Contour Lines.

Do you want your work published?

You can submit any work made using our prompts to our annual anthologies! Published submissions receive shared 25% royalties.

You can find more information on our website, www.TCStudiosHQ.com.

\#252 – Fitted Cap. (G) (M) (I)

Brainstorm …

- What material is it?
- What color is it?
- Does it have any patterns?
- How is it being worn?
- Is it hanging up/folded/tossed about?
- What condition is it in?
- Are there any features/interesting designs?

Brainstorm …

- Challenge: No Linework.
    - Try drawing this scene with no outlining – just dive right in with blocks of color!

Did you know?

A percentage of every anthology sold goes towards helping communities like yours. This includes donations to charities, funding of scholarships, creating of programs, and more!

You can find more information on our website, www.TCStudiosHQ.com.

258

#253 – Beanie. (G) (AP) (W)

Brainstorm …

- What material is it?
- What color is it?
- Does it have any patterns?
- How is it being worn?
- Is it hanging up/folded/tossed about?
- What condition is it in?
- Are there any features/interesting designs?

Brainstorm …

- Challenge: Continuous line.
    - Try drawing this scene with one continuous line.
    - You can color the finished image.

Did you know?

In addition to our annual prompt anthologies, every year we have themed anthologies that you can also submit to!

You can find more information on our website, www.TCStudiosHQ.com.

#254 – Graphic Tee. (C) (P) (CP)

Brainstorm …

- What material is it?
- What color is it?
- Does it have any patterns?
- How is it being worn?
- Is it hanging up/folded/tossed about?
- What condition is it in?
- Are there any features/interesting designs?

Brainstorm …

- Experiment: Colored Lighting.
  - When/if you are applying lighting effects to this piece, try using a different color instead of just a lighter gradient of the lit area.

Looking for a challenge?

Try doing one of our prompts with your friend(s)! See if you can come up with something together.

\#255 – Robe. (M) (I) (W)

Brainstorm …

- What material is it?
- What color is it?
- Does it have any patterns?
- How is it being worn?
- Is it hanging up/folded/tossed about?
- What condition is it in?
- Are there any features/interesting designs?

Brainstorm …

- Life Study.
    - Go out and find a person with this prompt to sketch.
    - See if someone you know will let you draw them!

Drawing Exercise #51

Draw an outfit with a witchy aesthetic.

261

\#256 – Dress. (AP) (P) (G)

Brainstorm …

- What material is it?
- What color is it?
- Does it have any patterns?
- How is it being worn?
- Is it hanging up/folded/tossed about?
- What condition is it in?
- Are there any features/interesting designs?

Brainstorm …

- Focus on: Realism.
  - o Try making the subject material for this prompt look as realistic as you can.

Did you know?

We also make books to help with storytelling. With help on things like creating characters, world-building, magic systems, and more!

You can find more information on our website, www.TCStudiosHQ.com.

#257 – Swimsuit. (C) (M) (W)

Brainstorm …

- What material is it?
- What color is it?
- Does it have any patterns?
- How is it being worn?
- Is it hanging up/folded/tossed about?
- What condition is it in?
- Are there any features/interesting designs?

Brainstorm …

- Practice: Skin Tones.
    - Study skin tone palettes and techniques and implement them in your drawing.

Did you know?

We also publish novels and comics that you can read!

You can find more information on our website,
www.TCStudiosHQ.com.

#258 – Onesie. (I) (CP) (G)

Brainstorm …

- What material is it?
- What color is it?
- Does it have any patterns?
- How is it being worn?
- Is it hanging up/folded/tossed about?
- What condition is it in?
- Are there any features/interesting designs?

Brainstorm …

- Challenge: No references.
  - Put your muscle memory to the test and draw this scene without using any references.
    - Good luck!

Do you want to give us a prompt for next year's edition?

You can submit prompt ideas you have based on next year's chapter themes. Credit will be given if selected.

You can find more information on our website, www.TCStudiosHQ.com.

\#259 – Pencil Skirt. (P) (W) (C)

Brainstorm …

- What material is it?
- What color is it?
- Does it have any patterns?
- How is it being worn?
- Is it hanging up/folded/tossed about?
- What condition is it in?
- Are there any features/interesting designs?

Brainstorm …

- Challenge: Monochrome.
  - Try drawing this scene using only one gradient of color.

Did you know?

We post daily writing & drawing prompts on our Social Medias for everyone to participate in.

Find us @PromptParty and use #PromptParty.

You can find more information on our website, www.TCStudiosHQ.com.

#260 – Blouse. (AP) (G) (I)

Brainstorm …

- What material is it?
- What color is it?
- Does it have any patterns?
- How is it being worn?
- Is it hanging up/folded/tossed about?
- What condition is it in?
- Are there any features/interesting designs?

Brainstorm …

- Challenge: Continuous line.
  - Try drawing this scene with one continuous line.
  - You can color the finished image.

Drawing Exercise #52

Draw an outfit with a professional aesthetic.

#261 – Stockings. (CP) (M) (C)

Brainstorm …

- What material is it?
- What color is it?
- Does it have any patterns?
- How is it being worn?
- Is it hanging up/folded/tossed about?
- What condition is it in?
- Are there any features/interesting designs?

Brainstorm …

- Practice: Anatomy.
  - Study proportions, positioning, and structure techniques and implement them in your drawing.

Did you know?

In addition to posting daily on Social Media, we have daily interactive posts on our YouTube channel, Podcast, and Blog.

You can find more information on our website, www.TCStudiosHQ.com.

#262 – Jumpsuit. (W) (AP) (P)

Brainstorm ...

- What material is it?
- What color is it?
- Does it have any patterns?
- How is it being worn?
- Is it hanging up/folded/tossed about?
- What condition is it in?
- Are there any features/interesting designs?

Brainstorm ...

- Experiment: Bold Line Work.
  - When you've finished lining your work (if you're lining), try making some areas thicker than others.
    - It can be dramatically, or just a bit.
      - Take note of how it changes the tone of your work.

Remember!

The listed genres/mediums and brainstorming boxes are **only suggestions!** We encourage you to do/use whatever you want.

\#263 – Winter Coat. (M) (I) (G)

Brainstorm …

- What material is it?
- What color is it?
- Does it have any patterns?
- How is it being worn?
- Is it hanging up/folded/tossed about?
- What condition is it in?
- Are there any features/interesting designs?

Brainstorm …

- Focus on: Background.
  - Tell the story with the use of the background and its environment. Think about the use and placement of specific items to help get the point across.

Be The First To Know.

Join our newsletter and be the first to know about new prompt books, novels, comics, giveaways, freebies, coupons, and anything else we've got going on!

Find our newsletter on our website, www.TCStudiosHQ.com.

\#264 – Vest. (P) (CP) (AP)

Brainstorm …

- What material is it?
- What color is it?
- Does it have any patterns?
- How is it being worn?
- Is it hanging up/folded/tossed about?
- What condition is it in?
- Are there any features/interesting designs?

Brainstorm (Drawing) …

- Practice: Texture.
  - Study texture techniques and implement them in your drawing.

You can share your work with us on Facebook, Instagram & Twitter!

Tag us @PromptParty and use #PromptParty.

We'd love to see what you come up with!

#265 – Sneakers. (W) (G) (C)

Brainstorm ...

- What material is it?
- What color is it?
- Does it have any patterns?
- How is it being worn?
- Is it hanging up/folded/tossed about?
- What condition is it in?
- Are there any features/interesting designs?

Brainstorm ...

- Challenge: Secondary Colors.
    - Try drawing this scene using only secondary colors and their gradients.

Drawing Exercise #53

Draw an outfit with an athletic aesthetic.

271

#266 – Sandals. (M) (AP) (P)

Brainstorm …

- What material is it?
- What color is it?
- Does it have any patterns?
- How is it being worn?
- Is it hanging up/folded/tossed about?
- What condition is it in?
- Are there any features/interesting designs?

Brainstorm …

- Challenge: No references.
  - Put your muscle memory to the test and draw this scene without using any references.
    - Good luck!

Do you want your work published?

You can submit any work made using our prompts to our annual anthologies! Published submissions receive shared 25% royalties.

You can find more information on our website, www.TCStudiosHQ.com.

#267 – Scarf. (I) (CP) (W)

Brainstorm …

- What material is it?
- What color is it?
- Does it have any patterns?
- How is it being worn?
- Is it hanging up/folded/tossed about?
- What condition is it in?
- Are there any features/interesting designs?

Brainstorm …

- Challenge: Self-Portrait.
    - o Draw yourself into this scene.

Did you know?

A percentage of every anthology sold goes towards helping communities like yours. This includes donations to charities, funding of scholarships, creating of programs, and more!

You can find more information on our website, www.TCStudiosHQ.com.

#268 – Button-up. (G) (P) (M)

Brainstorm ...

- What material is it?
- What color is it?
- Does it have any patterns?
- How is it being worn?
- Is it hanging up/folded/tossed about?
- What condition is it in?
- Are there any features/interesting designs?

Brainstorm ...

- Practice: Hands.
  - Study up on some hand techniques and implement them in your drawing.
    - Maybe they're pushing their hand through the sleeve or buttoning the shirt up.

Did you know?

In addition to our annual prompt anthologies, every year we have <u>themed</u> anthologies that you can also submit to!

You can find more information on our website,
www.TCStudiosHQ.com.

\#269 – Crop Top. (AP) (C) (I)

Brainstorm …

- What material is it?
- What color is it?
- Does it have any patterns?
- How is it being worn?
- Is it hanging up/folded/tossed about?
- What condition is it in?
- Are there any features/interesting designs?

Brainstorm …

- Challenge: Input.
  - Let someone tell you how you should set up your drawing and follow their instructions to the best of your ability.

Looking for a challenge?

Try doing one of our prompts with your friend(s)! See if you can come up with something together.

#270 – Hoodie. (CP) (M) (W)

Brainstorm …

- What material is it?
- What color is it?
- Does it have any patterns?
- How is it being worn?
- Is it hanging up/folded/tossed about?
- What condition is it in?
- Are there any features/interesting designs?

Brainstorm …

- Experiment: Comic Strip.
    - Try drawing this as a short comic strip.

Drawing Exercise #54

Draw an outfit with a hipster aesthetic.

\#271 – Fedora. (P) (G) (I)

Brainstorm …

- What material is it?
- What color is it?
- Does it have any patterns?
- How is it being worn?
- Is it hanging up/folded/tossed about?
- What condition is it in?
- Are there any features/interesting designs?

Brainstorm …

- Practice: Hair.
    - Study the flow and lighting of hair and implement the techniques into your drawing.

Did you know?

We also make books to help with storytelling. With help on things like creating characters, world-building, magic systems, and more!

You can find more information on our website,
www.TCStudiosHQ.com.

\#272 – Leggings. (AP) (M) (C)

Brainstorm …

- What material is it?
- What color is it?
- Does it have any patterns?
- How is it being worn?
- Is it hanging up/folded/tossed about?
- What condition is it in?
- Are there any features/interesting designs?

Brainstorm …

- Challenge: Life Reference.
    - See if you can take your own reference photos to use in your drawing.

Did you know?

We also publish novels and comics that you can read!

You can find more information on our website,
www.TCStudiosHQ.com.

#273 – Boots. (CP) (P) (W)

Brainstorm …

- What material is it?
- What color is it?
- Does it have any patterns?
- How is it being worn?
- Is it hanging up/folded/tossed about?
- What condition is it in?
- Are there any features/interesting designs?

Brainstorm …

- Practice: Lighting.
  - Study color choice, gradients, and placement techniques of lighting and implement them in your drawing.

Do you want to give us a prompt for next year's edition?

You can submit prompt ideas you have based on next year's chapter themes. Credit will be given if selected.

You can find more information on our website, www.TCStudiosHQ.com.

#274 – Sweater. (I) (AP) (G)

Brainstorm …

- What material is it?
- What color is it?
- Does it have any patterns?
- How is it being worn?
- Is it hanging up/folded/tossed about?
- What condition is it in?
- Are there any features/interesting designs?

Brainstorm …

- Focus on: Storyline.
  - Can you tell a story using this prompt?

Did you know?

We post daily writing & drawing prompts on our Social Medias for everyone to participate in.

Find us @PromptParty and use #PromptParty.

You can find more information on our website, www.TCStudiosHQ.com.

#275 – Nude. (M) (CP) (C)

Brainstorm ...

- Why?
  - o Are they bathing?
  - o Are they being intimate?
  - o Are they modeling?
  - o Are they a nudist?
- How do they feel about it?
  - o Confident?
  - o Self-conscious?
  - o Indifferent?

Brainstorm ...

- Challenge: No Linework.
  - o Try drawing this scene with no outlining – just dive right in with blocks of color!

Drawing Exercise #55

Draw an outfit with a nerdy aesthetic.

Chapter Ten: Self-Care.

#276 – Bubble Bath. (AP) (W) (I)

Brainstorm …

- What color are the bubbles?
- What does the bathroom look like?
- Are there any plants?
- Are they doing anything while bathing?

Brainstorm …

- Challenge: Continuous line.
    - Try drawing this scene with one continuous line.
    - You can color the finished image.

Did you know?

In addition to posting daily on Social Media, we have daily interactive posts on our YouTube channel, Podcast, and Blog.

You can find more information on our website, www.TCStudiosHQ.com.

#277 – Face Mask. (P) (C) (G)

Brainstorm …

- What kind?
- Does it wash or peel off?
- Are they doing anything while they wait?
- Is it at home or professional?
- What color is the mask?

Brainstorm …

- Challenge: Bird's Eye View.
    o Try drawing this piece with a bird's eye view.

Remember!

The listed genres/mediums and brainstorming boxes are **only suggestions!** We encourage you to do/use whatever you want.

283

#278 – Nap Time. (CP) (M) (I)

Brainstorm …

- Is there any white noise playing?
- Are they sleeping with a blanket?
- Are they sleeping with a stuffed animal?
- What are they wearing?
- Are they napping with anyone else?
- Where are they napping?

Brainstorm …

- Practice different types of shading techniques.
    - Hatching.
    - Cross-Hatching.
    - Stippling.
    - Scribbling.
    - Contour Lines.

Be The First To Know.

Join our newsletter and be the first to know about new prompt books, novels, comics, giveaways, freebies, coupons, and anything else we've got going on!

Find our newsletter on our website, www.TCStudiosHQ.com.

#279 – Cuddles. (AP) (G) (C)

Brainstorm …

- With whom?
  - Partner?
  - Pet?
  - Parent?
  - Stuffed animal?

Brainstorm …

- Challenge: Color Palette.
  - Use a random color palette generator or ask a friend to pick 3-5 colors for you to use.

You can share your work with us on Facebook, Instagram & Twitter!

Tag us @PromptParty and use #PromptParty.

We'd love to see what you come up with!

#280 – Movies. (P) (W) (CP)

Brainstorm …

- What genre?
- How long is it?
- Is it animated?
- Is it a series?

Brainstorm …

- Experiment: Colored Lighting.
  - When/if you are applying lighting effects to this piece, try using a different color instead of just a lighter gradient of the lit area.

Drawing Exercise #56

Draw 5 items involved in a spa day.

#281 – Meditation. (M) (I) (G)

Brainstorm …

- For how long?
- Are they experienced?
- How do they go about mediating?

Brainstorm …

- Focus on: Body Language.
  - How can you position the body to emphasize this prompt?

Do you want your work published?

You can submit any work made using our prompts to our annual anthologies! Published submissions receive shared 25% royalties.

You can find more information on our website, www.TCStudiosHQ.com.

#282 – Painting Nails. (C) (I) (AP)

Brainstorm …

- What color?
- Are there any designs?
- How long are they?
- Are they square? Pointed? Round?
- Is there acrylic?
- Is it gel or regular polish?

Brainstorm …

- Focus on: Background.
  - Tell the story with the use of the background and its environment. Think about the use and placement of specific items to help get the point across.

Did you know?

A percentage of every anthology sold goes towards helping communities like yours. This includes donations to charities, funding of scholarships, creating of programs, and more!

You can find more information on our website, www.TCStudiosHQ.com.

\#283 – Take A Walk. (P) (CP) (W)

Brainstorm ...

- Where?
- For how long?
- What's the weather like?
- Are they alone?
- What's going on around them?

Brainstorm (Drawing) ...

- Challenge: Opposite Colors.
    - Pick a color and it's opposite (ex: red and green).
    - Try coloring this piece with only those two colors and their gradients.

Did you know?

In addition to our annual prompt anthologies, every year we have <u>themed</u> anthologies that you can also submit to!

You can find more information on our website, www.TCStudiosHQ.com.

#284 – Declutter. (I) (M) (G)

Brainstorm …

- What are they decluttering?
- Is it going well or poorly?
- What does the space look like?
    - Before?
    - During?
    - After?

Brainstorm …

- Experiment: Comic Strip.
    - Try drawing this as a short comic strip.

Looking for a challenge?

Try doing one of our prompts with your friend(s)! See if you can
come up with something together.

#285 – Hang out with a friend. (AP) (P) (W)

Brainstorm ...

- Where?
- What are they doing?

Brainstorm ...

- Life Study.
    - Go out and find a person with this prompt to sketch.
    - See if someone you know will let you draw them!

Drawing Exercise #57

Draw 5 items involved with taking a nap.

\#286 – Massage. (C) (G) (I)

Brainstorm …

- Where?
- For how long?
- By whom?
- Are they using any lotion or oil?

Brainstorm …

- Challenge: Monochrome.
    - Try drawing this scene using only one gradient of color.

Did you know?

We also make books to help with storytelling. With help on things like creating characters, world-building, magic systems, and more!

You can find more information on our website,
www.TCStudiosHQ.com.

\#287 – Exercise. (CP) (M) (W)

Brainstorm …

- What kind?
- Is there a focus area?
- For how long?
- What outfit are they using?

Brainstorm …

- Practice: Skin Tones.
  - Study skin tone palettes and techniques and implement them in your drawing.

Did you know?

We also publish novels and comics that you can read!

You can find more information on our website,
www.TCStudiosHQ.com.

#288 – Favorite Meal. (P) (AP) (G)

Brainstorm …

- What is it?
- How is it cooked?
- How is it eaten?
- What goes into it?

Brainstorm …

- Challenge: Continuous line.
  - Try drawing this scene with one continuous line.
  - You can color the finished image.

Do you want to give us a prompt for next year's edition?

You can submit prompt ideas you have based on next year's chapter themes. Credit will be given if selected.

You can find more information on our website,
www.TCStudiosHQ.com.

#289 – Diary Entry. (CP) (I) (W)

Brainstorm ...

- Are they happy?
- Are they venting?
- Is this new for them?
  - Have they been doing it for a while?
- Is it a bullet journal?
- Is it decorated?

Brainstorm ...

- Experiment: Bold Line Work.
  - When you've finished lining your work (if you're lining), try making some areas thicker than others.
    - It can be dramatically, or just a bit.
      - Take note of how it changes the tone of your work.

Did you know?

We post daily writing & drawing prompts on our Social Medias for everyone to participate in.

Find us @PromptParty and use #PromptParty.

You can find more information on our website, www.TCStudiosHQ.com.

#290 – Create. (M) (P) (C)

Brainstorm ...

- Create what?
- With what?
- Is it physical?
- Does it involve other people?

Brainstorm ...

- Challenge: No references.
    - o Put your muscle memory to the test and draw this scene without using any references.
        - Good luck!

Drawing Exercise #58

Draw 5 items involved with preparing your favorite meal.

#291 – Mantra. (W) (AP) (I)

<table>
<tr><td>

Brainstorm …

- Do they write it down?
- Do they say it to themselves?
  - Do they sing it?
  - Whisper it?
  - Think it?

</td></tr>
</table>

<table>
<tr><td>

Brainstorm …

- Practice: Lighting.
  - Study color choice, gradients, and placement techniques of lighting and implement them in your drawing.

</td></tr>
</table>

Did you know?

In addition to posting daily on Social Media, we have daily interactive posts on our YouTube channel, Podcast, and Blog.

You can find more information on our website, www.TCStudiosHQ.com.

\#292 – Bird Watching. (P) (CP) (G)

Brainstorm …

- What kinds of birds do they see?
- Where?
- Are they using binoculars?
- Are they taking pictures?
- Are they sketching them?

Brainstorm …

- Practice: Anatomy.
    - Study proportions, positioning, and structure techniques and implement them in your drawing.

Remember!

The listed genres/mediums and brainstorming boxes are **only suggestions!** We encourage you to do/use whatever you want.

#293 – Nostalgia. (I) (W) (M)

Brainstorm …

- From what?
  - Music?
  - People?
  - Television shows?
  - Movies?
  - Cartoons?
  - Old toys/items?

Brainstorm …

- Challenge: Self-Portrait.
  - Draw yourself into this scene.

Be The First To Know.

Join our newsletter and be the first to know about new prompt books, novels, comics, giveaways, freebies, coupons, and anything else we've got going on!

Find our newsletter on our website, www.TCStudiosHQ.com.

#294 – Family Time. (C) (P) (AP)

Brainstorm …

- With whom?
- Doing what?
- Where?

Brainstorm …

- Focus on: Storyline.
  - Can you tell a story using this prompt?

You can share your work with us on Facebook, Instagram & Twitter!

Tag us @PromptParty and use #PromptParty.

We'd love to see what you come up with!

\#295 – Cloud Watching. (G) (M) (CP)

<table>
<tr><td>

Brainstorm ...

- Where?
  - o Inside or outside?
- What shapes are they in?
- Are they drawing or sketching them?
- Are they taking pictures?

</td></tr>
</table>

<table>
<tr><td>

Brainstorm ...

- Challenge: No Linework.
  - o Try drawing this scene with no outlining – just dive right in with blocks of color!

</td></tr>
</table>

<table>
<tr><td>

Drawing Exercise #59

Draw 5 items involved with having a movie night.

</td></tr>
</table>

#296 – New Place. (I) (W) (AP)

<table>
<tr><td>

Brainstorm …

- Where?
- How do you get there?
- What do you do there?
- What does it look like?

</td></tr>
</table>

<table>
<tr><td>

Brainstorm …

- Challenge: Secondary Colors.
  - o Try drawing this scene using only secondary colors and their gradients.

</td></tr>
</table>

Do you want your work published?

You can submit any work made using our prompts to our annual anthologies! Published submissions receive shared 25% royalties.

You can find more information on our website,
www.TCStudiosHQ.com.

#297 – Favorite Activity. (M) (C) (P)

Brainstorm …

- What do you do?
- How?
- What is the result?
- Do you do it alone?
- Does it involve other people?

Brainstorm (Drawing) …

- Practice: Texture.
    - Study texture techniques and implement them in your drawing.

Did you know?

A percentage of every anthology sold goes towards helping communities like yours. This includes donations to charities, funding of scholarships, creating of programs, and more!

You can find more information on our website, www.TCStudiosHQ.com.

\#298 – Doodle. (CP) (G) (I)

<table>
<tr><td>

Brainstorm …

- Of what?
- Using what?
- On what?
  - Paper?
  - Computer?

</td></tr>
</table>

<table>
<tr><td>

Brainstorm …

- Practice: Hands.
  - Study up on some hand techniques and implement them in your drawing.
    - Maybe they're holding or sharpening a pencil.

</td></tr>
</table>

Did you know?

In addition to our annual prompt anthologies, every year we have <u>themed</u> anthologies that you can also submit to!

You can find more information on our website,
www.TCStudiosHQ.com.

#299 – Favorite Music. (P) (W) (C)

Brainstorm …

- What genre?
- Do they play any of the instruments involved?
- Are they dancing?
- Are they relaxing?
- Are they doing something else while listening?

Brainstorm …

- Challenge: Bird's Eye View.
    - Try drawing this piece with a bird's eye view.

Looking for a challenge?

Try doing one of our prompts with your friend(s)! See if you can come up with something together.

\#300 – Treat Yourself. (M) (AP) (G)

Brainstorm …

- With what?
- What does it entail?
- Does it involve other people?

Brainstorm …

- Experiment: Comic Strip.
    - Try drawing this as a short comic strip.

Drawing Exercise #60

Draw 5 items involved with playing games.

#301 – Gratitude List. (C) (I) (CP)

Brainstorm …

- What is it on?
    - Sticky note?
    - Journal?
    - Phone?
- How many items are on the list?
    - Are they thinking of more?
- Is the list kept somewhere they can see it?

Brainstorm …

- Challenge: Secondary Colors.
    - Try drawing this scene using only secondary colors and their gradients.

Did you know?

We also make books to help with storytelling. With help on things like creating characters, world-building, magic systems, and more!

You can find more information on our website, www.TCStudiosHQ.com.

#302 – Unplug. (P) (W) (AP)

Brainstorm ...

- From what?
- What are they doing instead?

Brainstorm ...

- Focus on: Background.
    - Tell the story with the use of the background and its environment. Think about the use and placement of specific items to help get the point across.

Did you know?

We also publish novels and comics that you can read!

You can find more information on our website,
www.TCStudiosHQ.com.

\#303 – Coloring Book. (G) (CP) (I)

Brainstorm …

- What is the theme of the book?
- Are they just starting it?
    - Is it partially completed?
- What medium are they using?
    - Color pencil?
    - Marker?
    - Crayon?

Brainstorm …

- Challenge: Input.
    - Let someone tell you how you should set up your drawing and follow their instructions to the best of your ability.

Do you want to give us a prompt for next year's edition?

You can submit prompt ideas you have based on next year's chapter themes. Credit will be given if selected.

You can find more information on our website, www.TCStudiosHQ.com.

\#304 – Favorite Dessert. (P) (C) (M)

Brainstorm …   310

- What is it?
- Can it be eaten with your hands?
- Is it served hot or cold?

Brainstorm …

- Challenge: Life Reference.
  - See if you can take your own reference photos to use in your drawing.

Did you know?

We post daily writing & drawing prompts on our Social Medias for everyone to participate in.

Find us @PromptParty and use #PromptParty.

You can find more information on our website, www.TCStudiosHQ.com.

#305 – Hair. (I) (AP) (W)

Brainstorm ...

- What color is it?
- Is it long or short?
- Is it styled?
- Are they washing it?
- Are they coloring it?
- Are they cutting it?

Brainstorm ...

- Challenge: Continuous line.
  - o Try drawing this scene with one continuous line.
  - o You can color the finished image.

Drawing Exercise #61

Draw 5 items involved with doing your hair.

Chapter Eleven: Colors.

#306 – Teal. (CP) (P) (G)

Brainstorm …

- What gradient(s) are being used?
- Is it muted or amplified?
- Is it blended with anything else?
- Where is this color seen often?
- Do you own anything this color?

Brainstorm …

- Focus on: Realism.
    - Try making the subject material for this prompt look as realistic as you can.

Did you know?

In addition to posting daily on Social Media, we have daily interactive posts on our YouTube channel, Podcast, and Blog.

You can find more information on our website,
www.TCStudiosHQ.com.

\#307 – Yellow. (C) (I) (W)

Brainstorm ...

- What gradient(s) are being used?
- Is it muted or amplified?
- Is it blended with anything else?
- Where is this color seen often?
- Do you own anything this color?

Brainstorm ...

- Practice different types of shading techniques.
  - Hatching.
  - Cross-Hatching.
  - Stippling.
  - Scribbling.
  - Contour Lines.

Remember!

The listed genres/mediums and brainstorming boxes are **only suggestions!** We encourage you to do/use whatever you want.

#308 – Burgundy. (M) (AP) (CP)

Brainstorm …

- What gradient(s) are being used?
- Is it muted or amplified?
- Is it blended with anything else?
- Where is this color seen often?
- Do you own anything this color?

Brainstorm …

- Practice: Anatomy.
    - Study proportions, positioning, and structure techniques and implement them in your drawing.

Be The First To Know.

Join our newsletter and be the first to know about new prompt books, novels, comics, giveaways, freebies, coupons, and anything else we've got going on!

Find our newsletter on our website, www.TCStudiosHQ.com.

#309 – Lime Green. (I) (P) (C)

Brainstorm …

- What gradient(s) are being used?
- Is it muted or amplified?
- Is it blended with anything else?
- Where is this color seen often?
- Do you own anything this color?

Brainstorm …

- Experiment: Bold Line Work.
  - When you've finished lining your work (if you're lining), try making some areas thicker than others.
    - It can be dramatically, or just a bit.
      - Take note of how it changes the tone of your work.

You can share your work with us on Facebook, Instagram & Twitter!

Tag us @PromptParty and use #PromptParty.

We'd love to see what you come up with!

#310 – Pine Green. (W) (M) (AP)

<table>
<tr><td>

Brainstorm …

- What gradient(s) are being used?
- Is it muted or amplified?
- Is it blended with anything else?
- Where is this color seen often?
- Do you own anything this color?

</td></tr>
</table>

<table>
<tr><td>

Brainstorm …

- Challenge: Bird's Eye View.
  - Try drawing this piece with a bird's eye view.

</td></tr>
</table>

<table>
<tr><td>

Drawing Exercise #62

Draw 10 things that are primarily red.

</td></tr>
</table>

#311 – Royal Blue. (CP) (C) (P)

Brainstorm ...

- What gradient(s) are being used?
- Is it muted or amplified?
- Is it blended with anything else?
- Where is this color seen often?
- Do you own anything this color?

Brainstorm ...

- Practice: Hair.
  - Study the flow and lighting dimensions of hair and implement the techniques into your drawing.

Do you want your work published?

You can submit any work made using our prompts to our annual anthologies! Published submissions receive shared 25% royalties.

You can find more information on our website, www.TCStudiosHQ.com.

#312 – Orange. (M) (I) (G)

Brainstorm …

- What gradient(s) are being used?
- Is it muted or amplified?
- Is it blended with anything else?
- Where is this color seen often?
- Do you own anything this color?

Brainstorm …

- Challenge: No references.
    - Put your muscle memory to the test and draw this scene without using any references.
        - Good luck!

Did you know?

A percentage of every anthology sold goes towards helping communities like yours. This includes donations to charities, funding of scholarships, creating of programs, and more!

You can find more information on our website, www.TCStudiosHQ.com.

\#313 – Violet. (P) (AP) (W)

Brainstorm ...

- What gradient(s) are being used?
- Is it muted or amplified?
- Is it blended with anything else?
- Where is this color seen often?
- Do you own anything this color?

Brainstorm ...

- Practice: Lighting.
    - Study color choice, gradients, and placement techniques of lighting and implement them in your drawing.

Did you know?

In addition to our annual prompt anthologies, every year we have <u>themed</u> anthologies that you can also submit to!

You can find more information on our website, www.TCStudiosHQ.com.

#314 – Pink. (C) (M) (CP)

Brainstorm …

- What gradient(s) are being used?
- Is it muted or amplified?
- Is it blended with anything else?
- Where is this color seen often?
- Do you own anything this color?

Brainstorm …

- Experiment: Comic Strip.
  - Try drawing this as a short comic strip.

Looking for a challenge?

Try doing one of our prompts with your friend(s)! See if you can
come up with something together.

#315 – Red-Orange. (W) (G) (I)

Brainstorm …

- What gradient(s) are being used?
- Is it muted or amplified?
- Is it blended with anything else?
- Where is this color seen often?
- Do you own anything this color?

Brainstorm …

- Practice: Anatomy.
  - Study proportions, positioning, and structure techniques and implement them in your drawing.

Drawing Exercise #63

Draw 10 things that are primarily blue.

#316 – Mustard. (AP) (M) (P)

Brainstorm …

- What gradient(s) are being used?
- Is it muted or amplified?
- Is it blended with anything else?
- Where is this color seen often?
- Do you own anything this color?

Brainstorm …

- Challenge: Continuous line.
  - Try drawing this scene with one continuous line.
  - You can color the finished image.

Did you know?

We also make books to help with storytelling. With help on things like creating characters, world-building, magic systems, and more!

You can find more information on our website, www.TCStudiosHQ.com.

#317 – Brown. (W) (C) (I)

Brainstorm …

- What gradient(s) are being used?
- Is it muted or amplified?
- Is it blended with anything else?
- Where is this color seen often?
- Do you own anything this color?

Brainstorm …

- Challenge: Monochrome.
  - Try drawing this scene using only one gradient of color.

Did you know?

We also publish novels and comics that you can read!

You can find more information on our website,
www.TCStudiosHQ.com.

#318 – Pastel. (G) (CP) (M)

Brainstorm ...   324

- What gradient(s) are being used?
- Is it muted or amplified?
- Is it blended with anything else?
- Where is this color seen often?
- Do you own anything this color?

Brainstorm ...

- Challenge: Self-Portrait.
    - Draw yourself into this scene.

Do you want to give us a prompt for next year's edition?

You can submit prompt ideas you have based on next year's chapter themes. Credit will be given if selected.

You can find more information on our website, www.TCStudiosHQ.com.

\#319 – White. (I) (P) (AP)

Brainstorm ...

- What gradient(s) are being used?
- Is it muted or amplified?
- Is it blended with anything else?
- Where is this color seen often?
- Do you own anything this color?

Brainstorm ...

- Experiment: Colored Lighting.
  - When/if you are applying lighting effects to this piece, try using a different color instead of just a lighter gradient of the lit area.

Did you know?

We post daily writing & drawing prompts on our Social Medias for everyone to participate in.

Find us @PromptParty and use #PromptParty.

You can find more information on our website, www.TCStudiosHQ.com.

#320 – Black. (W) (C) (G)

Brainstorm …

- What gradient(s) are being used?
- Is it muted or amplified?
- Is it blended with anything else?
- Where is this color seen often?
- Do you own anything this color?

Brainstorm …

- Challenge: No Linework.
  - Try drawing this scene with no outlining – just dive right in with blocks of color!

Drawing Exercise #64

Draw 10 things that are primarily yellow.

\#321 – Sky Blue. (CP) (P) (I)

Brainstorm …

- What gradient(s) are being used?
- Is it muted or amplified?
- Is it blended with anything else?
- Where is this color seen often?
- Do you own anything this color?

Brainstorm …

- Challenge: No references.
    - o Put your muscle memory to the test and draw this scene without using any references.
        - Good luck!

Did you know?

In addition to posting daily on Social Media, we have daily interactive posts on our YouTube channel, Podcast, and Blog.

You can find more information on our website,
www.TCStudiosHQ.com.

\#322 – Purple. (M) (W) (AP)

Brainstorm ...

- What gradient(s) are being used?
- Is it muted or amplified?
- Is it blended with anything else?
- Where is this color seen often?
- Do you own anything this color?

Brainstorm ...

- Practice different types of shading techniques.
  - Hatching.
  - Cross-Hatching.
  - Stippling.
  - Scribbling.
  - Contour Lines.

Remember!

The listed genres/mediums and brainstorming boxes are **only suggestions!** We encourage you to do/use whatever you want.

\#323 – Red. (C) (G) (I)

Brainstorm …

- What gradient(s) are being used?
- Is it muted or amplified?
- Is it blended with anything else?
- Where is this color seen often?
- Do you own anything this color?

Brainstorm …

- Challenge: Input.
  - Let someone tell you how you should set up your drawing and follow their instructions to the best of your ability.

Be The First To Know.

Join our newsletter and be the first to know about new prompt books, novels, comics, giveaways, freebies, coupons, and anything else we've got going on!

Find our newsletter on our website, www.TCStudiosHQ.com.

#324 – Mint Green. (P) (W) (CP)

Brainstorm …   330

- What gradient(s) are being used?
- Is it muted or amplified?
- Is it blended with anything else?
- Where is this color seen often?
- Do you own anything this color?

Brainstorm …

- Focus on: Storyline.
  - Can you tell a story using this prompt?

You can share your work with us on Facebook, Instagram & Twitter!

Tag us @PromptParty and use #PromptParty.

We'd love to see what you come up with!

#325 – Lilac Purple. (I) (AP) (G)

Brainstorm ...

- What gradient(s) are being used?
- Is it muted or amplified?
- Is it blended with anything else?
- Where is this color seen often?
- Do you own anything this color?

Brainstorm ...

- Practice: Texture.
  - o Study texture techniques and implement them in your drawing.

Drawing Exercise #65

Draw 10 things that are primarily black.

\#326 – Silver. (C) (M) (CP)

Brainstorm …

- What gradient(s) are being used?
- Is it muted or amplified?
- Is it blended with anything else?
- Where is this color seen often?
- Do you own anything this color?

Brainstorm …

- Experiment: Bold Line Work.
  - When you've finished lining your work (if you're lining), try making some areas thicker than others.
    - It can be dramatically, or just a bit.
      - Take note of how it changes the tone of your work.

Do you want your work published?

You can submit any work made using our prompts to our annual anthologies! Published submissions receive shared 25% royalties.

You can find more information on our website,
www.TCStudiosHQ.com.

#327 – Ivory. (AP) (P) (I)

<hr>

Brainstorm …

- What gradient(s) are being used?
- Is it muted or amplified?
- Is it blended with anything else?
- Where is this color seen often?
- Do you own anything this color?

<hr>

Brainstorm …

- Challenge: Continuous line.
  - Try drawing this scene with one continuous line.
  - You can color the finished image.

Did you know?

A percentage of every anthology sold goes towards helping communities like yours. This includes donations to charities, funding of scholarships, creating of programs, and more!

You can find more information on our website, www.TCStudiosHQ.com.

\#328 – Hazel. (W) (CP) (G)

Brainstorm …

- What gradient(s) are being used?
- Is it muted or amplified?
- Is it blended with anything else?
- Where is this color seen often?
- Do you own anything this color?

Brainstorm …

- Challenge: Life Reference.
  - See if you can take your own reference photos to use in your drawing.

Did you know?

In addition to our annual prompt anthologies, every year we have themed anthologies that you can also submit to!

You can find more information on our website, www.TCStudiosHQ.com.

#329 – Mocha. (P) (M) (C)

Brainstorm …

- What gradient(s) are being used?
- Is it muted or amplified?
- Is it blended with anything else?
- Where is this color seen often?
- Do you own anything this color?

Brainstorm …

- Practice: Skin Tones.
    - Study skin tone palettes and techniques and implement them in your drawing.

Looking for a challenge?

Try doing one of our prompts with your friend(s)! See if you can come up with something together.

#330 – Sea-Foam Green. (AP) (G) (I)

Brainstorm ...

- What gradient(s) are being used?
- Is it muted or amplified?
- Is it blended with anything else?
- Where is this color seen often?
- Do you own anything this color?

Brainstorm ...

- Practice: Hands.
  - Study up on some hand techniques and implement them in your drawing.
    - Maybe they're holding something this color or using this color in a drawing.

Drawing Exercise #66

Draw 10 things that are primarily green.

\#331 – Peach. (W) (CP) (M)

Brainstorm …

- What gradient(s) are being used?
- Is it muted or amplified?
- Is it blended with anything else?
- Where is this color seen often?
- Do you own anything this color?

Brainstorm (Drawing) …

- Practice: Texture.
    - Study texture techniques and implement them in your drawing.

Did you know?

We also make books to help with storytelling. With help on things like creating characters, world-building, magic systems, and more!

You can find more information on our website, www.TCStudiosHQ.com.

337

\#332 – Navy Blue. (C) (P) (AP)

<table>
<tr><td>

Brainstorm …

- What gradient(s) are being used?
- Is it muted or amplified?
- Is it blended with anything else?
- Where is this color seen often?
- Do you own anything this color?

</td></tr>
</table>

<table>
<tr><td>

Brainstorm …

- Challenge: No references.
  - o Put your muscle memory to the test and draw this scene without using any references.
    - Good luck!

</td></tr>
</table>

Did you know?

We also publish novels and comics that you can read!

You can find more information on our website,
www.TCStudiosHQ.com.

#333 – Taupe. (G) (CP) (I)

Brainstorm …

- What gradient(s) are being used?
- Is it muted or amplified?
- Is it blended with anything else?
- Where is this color seen often?
- Do you own anything this color?

Brainstorm …

- Focus on: Realism.
    - Try making the subject material for this prompt look as realistic as you can.

Do you want to give us a prompt for next year's edition?

You can submit prompt ideas you have based on next year's chapter themes. Credit will be given if selected.

You can find more information on our website, www.TCStudiosHQ.com.

#334 – Gold. (M) (P) (C)

<table>
<tr><td>

Brainstorm …

- What gradient(s) are being used?
- Is it muted or amplified?
- Is it blended with anything else?
- Where is this color seen often?
- Do you own anything this color?

</td></tr>
</table>

<table>
<tr><td>

Brainstorm …

- Practice: Lighting.
  - Study color choice, gradients, and placement techniques of lighting and implement them in your drawing.

</td></tr>
</table>

Did you know?

We post daily writing & drawing prompts on our Social Medias for everyone to participate in.

Find us @PromptParty and use #PromptParty.

You can find more information on our website, www.TCStudiosHQ.com.

#335 – Bronze. (AP) (G) (W)

Brainstorm …

- What gradient(s) are being used?
- Is it muted or amplified?
- Is it blended with anything else?
- Where is this color seen often?
- Do you own anything this color?

Brainstorm …

- Focus on: Storyline.
    - o   Can you tell a story using this prompt?

Drawing Exercise #67

Draw 10 things that are primarily white.

\#336 – Rainbow. (I) (CP) (P)

Brainstorm …

- What gradient(s) are being used?
- Is it muted or amplified?
- Is it blended with anything else?
- Where is this color seen often?
- Do you own anything this color?

Brainstorm …

- Practice: Hair.
  - Study the flow and lighting dimensions of hair and implement the techniques into your drawing.

Did you know?

In addition to posting daily on Social Media, we have daily interactive posts on our YouTube channel, Podcast, and Blog.

You can find more information on our website, www.TCStudiosHQ.com.

Chapter Twelve: Food & Beverages.

#337 – Dessert. (W) (AP) (I)

Brainstorm …

- Cake?
- Pie?
- Ice cream?
- Fruit?

Brainstorm …

- Challenge: Color Palette.
  - Use a random color palette generator or ask a friend to pick 3-5 colors for you to use.

Remember!

The listed genres/mediums and brainstorming boxes are **only suggestions!** We encourage you to do/use whatever you want.

343

#338 – Pizza. (M) (G) (C)

Brainstorm …

- Cheesy?
- White? Red?
- What kind of toppings?
- How big?
- What kind of crust?

Brainstorm …

- Experiment: Comic Strip.
  - Try drawing this as a short comic strip.

Be The First To Know.

Join our newsletter and be the first to know about new prompt books, novels, comics, giveaways, freebies, coupons, and anything else we've got going on!

Find our newsletter on our website, www.TCStudiosHQ.com.

\#339 – Milkshake. (P) (W) (AP)

Brainstorm …

- What flavor?
- Is there whipped cream?
- What kind of cup is it in?
- Is it being shared?

Brainstorm …

- Challenge: No references.
  - Put your muscle memory to the test and draw this scene without using any references.
    - Good luck!

You can share your work with us on Facebook, Instagram & Twitter!

Tag us @PromptParty and use #PromptParty.

We'd love to see what you come up with!

#340 – Tea. (G) (CP) (M)

Brainstorm …

- What flavor?
- With or without milk?
- Any sugar?
- What kind of cup is it in?
- Hot or cold?

Brainstorm …

- Challenge: No Linework.
    - Try drawing this scene with no outlining – just dive right in with blocks of color!

Drawing Exercise #68

Draw a plate of your favorite fruits.

#341 – Spaghetti. (C) (I) (P)

<table>
<tr><td>

Brainstorm …

- Does the sauce have meat?
- Are there meatballs?
- How thick is the pasta?
- Are there any other toppings?
    - Basil?
    - Parmesan?

</td></tr>
</table>

<table>
<tr><td>

Brainstorm …

- Challenge: Bird's Eye View.
    - Try drawing this piece with a bird's eye view.

</td></tr>
</table>

Do you want your work published?

You can submit any work made using our prompts to our annual anthologies! Published submissions receive shared 25% royalties.

You can find more information on our website,
www.TCStudiosHQ.com.

#342 – Sandwich. (M) (AP) (G)

Brainstorm ...

- What kind?
- What's in it?
- What kind of bread?
- Is it cut in half?
- How big is it?

Brainstorm ...

- Practice different types of shading techniques.
  - Hatching.
  - Cross-Hatching.
  - Stippling.
  - Scribbling.
  - Contour Lines.

Did you know?

A percentage of every anthology sold goes towards helping communities like yours. This includes donations to charities, funding of scholarships, creating of programs, and more!

You can find more information on our website, www.TCStudiosHQ.com.

#343 – Banana Pancakes. (CP) (W) (P)

Brainstorm …

- Butter?
- Syrup?
  - What kind?
- Served with what?
  - Eggs?
  - Bacon?
  - Toast?
  - Grits?

Brainstorm …

- Challenge: Continuous line.
  - Try drawing this scene with one continuous line.
  - You can color the finished image.

Did you know?

In addition to our annual prompt anthologies, every year we have
<u>themed</u> anthologies that you can also submit to!

You can find more information on our website,
www.TCStudiosHQ.com.

\#344 – Taco. (I) (M) (G)

Brainstorm …

- Chicken or beef?
- What's in it?
- Hard or soft?

Brainstorm …

- Practice: Hands.
    - Study up on some hand techniques and implement them in your drawing.
        - Maybe they're filling the taco or holding it to their mouth.

Looking for a challenge?

Try doing one of our prompts with your friend(s)! See if you can come up with something together.

#345 – Coffee. (C) (W) (AP)

Brainstorm ...

- What flavor?
  - Black?
  - Hazelnut?
- Is there milk/creamer?
- Is there sugar?
- Hot or cold?

Brainstorm ...

- Experiment: Colored Lighting.
  - When/if you are applying lighting effects to this piece, try using a different color instead of just a lighter gradient of the lit area.

Drawing Exercise #69

Draw a plate of your favorite vegetables.

\#346 – Water. (CP) (M) (I)

Brainstorm …

- Tap or filtered?
- Is it flavored?
- Does it have electrolytes?

Brainstorm …

- Challenge: Monochrome.
  - Try drawing this scene using only one gradient of color.

Did you know?

We also make books to help with storytelling. With help on things like creating characters, world-building, magic systems, and more!

You can find more information on our website,
www.TCStudiosHQ.com.

#347 – Bacon, Egg, & Cheese. (P) (G) (W)

Brainstorm …

- Salt, pepper, ketchup?
- Is it cut in half?
- Is it on a roll? Bagel? Toast?
- What kind of eggs?
- What kind of bacon?
- What kind of cheese?

Brainstorm …

- Practice: Texture.
  - Study texture techniques and implement them in your drawing.

Did you know?

We also publish novels and comics that you can read!

You can find more information on our website,
www.TCStudiosHQ.com.

#348 – Ice-cream. (M) (I) (AP)

Brainstorm …

- What flavor?
- How is it being used?
  - On a cone?
  - As a topping?
  - In a sundae?

Brainstorm …

- Experiment: Comic Strip.
  - Try drawing this as a short comic strip.

Do you want to give us a prompt for next year's edition?

You can submit prompt ideas you have based on next year's chapter themes. Credit will be given if selected.

You can find more information on our website, www.TCStudiosHQ.com.

#349 – French Fries. (CP) (C) (G)

Brainstorm …

- Are they straight or wavy?
- Do they have any toppings on them?
- Are they being served with anything?

Brainstorm …

- Challenge: Self-Portrait.
  - Draw yourself into this scene.

Did you know?

We post daily writing & drawing prompts on our Social Medias for everyone to participate in.

Find us @PromptParty and use #PromptParty.

You can find more information on our website,
www.TCStudiosHQ.com.

#350 – Cake. (W) (I) (P)

Brainstorm …

- What kind?
  - Vanilla?
  - Chocolate?
  - Cheesecake?
  - Fruit?
- Is it someone's birthday?
  - Is it a different celebration?
  - Is there writing on it?

Brainstorm …

- Focus on: Background.
  - Tell the story with the use of the background and its environment. Think about the use and placement of specific items to help get the point across.

Drawing Exercise #70

Draw 5 desserts that you like.

#351 – Carrots. (AP) (CP) (M)

Brainstorm …

- How are they prepared?
  - Steamed?
  - Grilled?
  - Raw?
- How big is it?
- Is it still growing?

Brainstorm …

- Challenge: No references.
  - Put your muscle memory to the test and draw this scene without using any references.
    - Good luck!

Did you know?

In addition to posting daily on Social Media, we have daily interactive posts on our YouTube channel, Podcast, and Blog.

You can find more information on our website, www.TCStudiosHQ.com.

#352 – Fried Rice. (C) (G) (P)

Brainstorm …

- What kind?
- What vegetables are in it?
- What meat is in it?
- Is it being served as a side or the main dish?

Brainstorm …

- Challenge: Secondary Colors.
  - Try drawing this scene using only secondary colors and their gradients.

Remember!

The listed genres/mediums and brainstorming boxes are **only suggestions!** We encourage you to do/use whatever you want.

#353 – Sushi. (I) (W) (M)

Brainstorm …

- What kind?
- What ingredients are there?
- Are there any cooked items?
- Is it being eaten with chopsticks?
- Is it being made fresh?

Brainstorm …

- Experiment: Bold Line Work.
  - When you've finished lining your work (if you're lining), try making some areas thicker than others.
    - It can be dramatically, or just a bit.
      - Take note of how it changes the tone of your work.

Be The First To Know.

Join our newsletter and be the first to know about new prompt books, novels, comics, giveaways, freebies, coupons, and anything else we've got going on!

Find our newsletter on our website, www.TCStudiosHQ.com.

#354 – Bubble Tea. (AP) (G) (C)

Brainstorm ...

- What flavor?
- What kind of cup is it in?
- Where did it come from?

Brainstorm ...

- Focus on: Storyline.
    - Can you tell a story using this prompt?

You can share your work with us on Facebook, Instagram & Twitter!

Tag us @PromptParty and use #PromptParty.

We'd love to see what you come up with!

#355 – Chips. (CP) (P) (I)

Brainstorm …

- Are they kettle cooked?
- Are they salted?
- Are they flavored?
- Are they being dipped in something?
- Are they being eaten with a meal?

Brainstorm …

- Practice different types of shading techniques.
    - Hatching.
    - Cross-Hatching.
    - Stippling.
    - Scribbling.
    - Contour Lines.

Drawing Exercise #71

Draw 5 breakfast items that you like.

\#356 – Muffin. (M) (AP) (W)

Brainstorm …

- What kind?
- Is it big or small?
- Is it wrapped or unwrapped?
- Is it homemade?
- Is there butter on it?

Brainstorm …

- Challenge: Continuous line.
  - Try drawing this scene with one continuous line.
  - You can color the finished image.

Do you want your work published?

You can submit any work made using our prompts to our annual anthologies! Published submissions receive shared 25% royalties.

You can find more information on our website, www.TCStudiosHQ.com.

#357 – Candy. (G) (P) (C)

Brainstorm …

- What kind?
  - Chocolate?
  - Peanut butter?
  - Fruity?
- Is it wrapped or unwrapped?
- Where is it?
  - A store?
  - In a basket?
  - In someone's hand?

Brainstorm …

- Experiment: Colored Lighting.
  - When/if you are applying lighting effects to this piece, try using a different color instead of just a lighter gradient of the lit area.

Did you know?

A percentage of every anthology sold goes towards helping communities like yours. This includes donations to charities, funding of scholarships, creating of programs, and more!

You can find more information on our website, www.TCStudiosHQ.com.

\#358 – Lemonade. (CP) (W) (AP)

Brainstorm …

- Is it plain or flavored?
- Is it sweet or sour?
- Is it being enjoyed on a hot day?
- Is there ice in it?
- Are there still lemons in it?

Brainstorm …

- Practice: Anatomy.
  - Study proportions, positioning, and structure techniques and implement them in your drawing.

Did you know?

In addition to our annual prompt anthologies, every year we have <u>themed</u> anthologies that you can also submit to!

You can find more information on our website, www.TCStudiosHQ.com.

\#359 – Salad. (M) (C) (I)

Brainstorm …

- What kind?
  - o Is there fruit?
  - o Are there vegetables?
  - o What dressing is being used?
- What is it being eaten with, if anything?
- Is the person on a diet?
- Are they vegan?

Brainstorm …

- Challenge: Input.
  - o Let someone tell you how you should set up your drawing and follow their instructions to the best of your ability.

Looking for a challenge?

Try doing one of our prompts with your friend(s)! See if you can come up with something together.

365

#360 – Mac & Cheese. (G) (P) (AP)

Brainstorm …

- Is it made from scratch or instant?
  - What kind of pasta?
  - What kind of cheese?
  - Is there anything added?
    - Bacon? Chili?

Brainstorm …

- Practice: Lighting.
  - Study color choice, gradients, and placement techniques of lighting and implement them in your drawing.

Drawing Exercise #72

Draw 5 beverages that you like.

#361 – Eggs. (CP) (I) (W)

Brainstorm ...

- Are they still in their shell?
    - Are they still around chickens?
    - Are they being collected?
- Are they being cooked?
    - How?
        - Scrambled, sunny side up, omelet?
    - Is there something being made with it?
    - Is it being used in something?
        - Baked goods?

Brainstorm ...

- Challenge: No Linework.
    - Try drawing this scene with no outlining – just dive right in with blocks of color!

Did you know?

We also make books to help with storytelling. With help on things like creating characters, world-building, magic systems, and more!

You can find more information on our website, www.TCStudiosHQ.com.

#362 – Steak. (P) (C) (AP)

Brainstorm …

- What kind of steak is it?
  - How is it made?
  - What seasonings are used?
  - Are any marinades used?
- What else is being prepared with it?
- How is it being prepared?

Brainstorm …

- Challenge: Continuous line.
  - Try drawing this scene with one continuous line.
  - You can color the finished image.

Did you know?

We also publish novels and comics that you can read!

You can find more information on our website,
www.TCStudiosHQ.com.

\#363 – Vegan. (M) (CP) (G)

Brainstorm …

- When did they make the decision to be vegan?
  - Why did they?
- What does their diet look like?
  - What are some of their favorite recipes?
- Are they offended by people that eat meat?
  - Are they tolerant?

Brainstorm …

- Challenge: Color Palette.
  - Use a random color palette generator or ask a friend to pick 3-5 colors for you to use.

Do you want to give us a prompt for next year's edition?

You can submit prompt ideas you have based on next year's chapter themes. Credit will be given if selected.

You can find more information on our website, www.TCStudiosHQ.com.

#364 – Hot Chocolate. (AP) (I) (P)

Brainstorm ...

- Is it plain or flavored?
- Is it made with milk or water?
- Are there marshmallows?
- Where is it being had?
    - By a fireplace?
    - In a café?
    - At a deli?
    - At home?

Brainstorm ...

- Experiment: Comic Strip.
    - Try drawing this as a short comic strip.

Did you know?

We post daily writing & drawing prompts on our Social Medias for everyone to participate in.

Find us @PromptParty and use #PromptParty.

You can find more information on our website, www.TCStudiosHQ.com.

#365 – Ramen. (C) (W) (CP)

Brainstorm …

- What flavor is it?
  - What toppings are sprinkled along the top?
- Where is it being eaten?
  - By whom?
  - Are they enjoying it?
  - Are they alone or with friends/family?
- Is it being eaten with chopsticks?

Brainstorm …

- Challenge: Bird's Eye View.
  - Try drawing this piece with a bird's eye view.

Drawing Exercise #73

Draw 5 snacks that you like.

Prompts by Medium

Pencil (P)

1. #3 – Mountain.
2. #7 – Tiny House.
3. #10 – Child.
4. #12 – Hero/Heroine.
5. #17 – Band.
6. #19 – Model.
7. #25 – Circus.
8. #27 – Athlete.
9. #30 – Dungeon.
10. #33 – Dry.
11. #35 – Soft.
12. #37 – Rough.
13. #38 – Fuzzy.
14. #40 – Slick.
15. #43 – Cracked.
16. #46 – Hairy.
17. #54 – Stretchy.
18. #56 – Wooden.
19. #59 – Silicone.
20. #60 – Canvas.
21. #65 – Pin-up.
22. #67 – Break Dancing.
23. #73 – Sneaking.
24. #75 – Kissing.
25. #77 – Playing.
26. #79 – Standing.
27. #83 – Tiptoeing.
28. #87 – Fighting.
29. #93 – Turtle.
30. #97 – Chicken.
31. #101 – Wolf.
32. #103 – Whale.
33. #109 – Phoenix.
34. #111 – Hummingbird.

35. #114 – Monkey.
36. #117 – Goat.
37. #120 – Chipmunk.
38. #124 – Pumpkin.
39. #127 – Jasmine.
40. #130 – Vines.
41. #132 – Rubber Plant.
42. #138 – Aloe Vera.
43. #141 – Lily Pad.
44. #143 – Fern.
45. #147 – Green Onion.
46. #150 – Philodendron.
47. #157 – Television.
48. #159 – Car.
49. #161 – iPod.
50. #163 – Hair Dryer.
51. #166 – Headphones.
52. #168 – Console Game.
53. #170 – Train.
54. #172 – Hearing Aid.
55. #175 – Remote.
56. #176 – GPS.
57. #178 – Tracker.
58. #180 – Refrigerator.
59. #183 – Robotic Limb.
60. #185 – Enraged.
61. #188 – Joyful.
62. #191 – Anxious.
63. #193 – Hyper.
64. #195 – Boredom.
65. #198 – Sleepy.
66. #201 – Guilty.
67. #204 – Lonely.
68. #206 – Stressed.
69. #208 – Curious.
70. #210 – Skeptical.
71. #213 – Nostalgic.
72. #215 – Potion.
73. #217 – Wizard.
74. #220 – Brewing Pot.

75. #223 – Potion Ingredients.
76. #225 – Magic School.
77. #227 – Witch's Hat.
78. #230 – Earth Witch/Wizard.
79. #233 – Sorcerer.
80. #235 – Spell Book.
81. #239 – Magical Boy.
82. #241 – Witch/Wizard's Home.
83. #243 – Scroll Shop.
84. #245 – Cardigan.
85. #250 – Romper.
86. #254 – Graphic Tee.
87. #256 – Dress.
88. #259 – Pencil Skirt.
89. #262 – Jumpsuit.
90. #264 – Vest.
91. #266 – Sandals.
92. #268 – Button-up.
93. #271 – Fedora.
94. #273 – Boots.
95. #277 – Face Mask.
96. #280 – Movies.
97. #283 – Take A Walk.
98. #285 – Hang Out w/ A Friend.
99. #288 – Favorite Meal.
100. #290 – Create.
101. #292 – Bird Watching.
102. #294 – Family Time.
103. #297 – Favorite Activity.
104. #299 – Favorite Music.
105. #302 – Unplug.
106. #304 – Favorite Dessert.
107. #306 – Teal.
108. #309 – Lime Green.
109. #311 – Royal Blue.
110. #313 – Violet.
111. #316 – Mustard.
112. #319 – White.
113. #321 – Sky Blue.
114. #324 – Mint Green.

115. #327 – Ivory.
116. #329 – Mocha.
117. #332 – Navy Blue.
118. #334 – Gold.
119. #336 – Rainbow.
120. #339 – Milkshake.
121. #341 – Spaghetti.
122. #343 – Banana Pancakes.
123. #347 – Bacon, Egg, & Cheese.
124. #350 – Cake.
125. #352 – Fried Rice.
126. #355 – Chips.
127. #357 – Candy.
128. #360 – Mac & Cheese.
129. #362 – Steak.
130. #364 – Hot Chocolate.

Color Pencil (CP)

1.   #1 – Ballerina.

2. #5 – Meadow.
3. #11 – Beach.
4. #13 – Witch.
5. #17 – Band.
6. #20 – Space.
7. #21 – Tropical Island.
8. #23 – House.
9. #26 – Artist.
10. #27 – Athlete.
11. #31 – Bookstore.
12. #32 – Slimy.
13. #34 – Wrinkled.
14. #38 – Fuzzy.
15. #40 – Slick.
16. #45 – Scratchy.
17. #47 – Gooey.
18. #50 – Metallic.
19. #52 – Jean.

20. #54 – Stretchy.
21. #58 – Plastic.
22. #62 – Sleeping.
23. #63 – Jumping.
24. #69 – Sliding.
25. #73 – Sneaking.
26. #76 – Rolling.
27. #79 – Standing.
28. #82 – Kicking.
29. #83 – Tiptoeing.
30. #86 – Blocking.
31. #88 – Praying.
32. #91 – Waving.
33. #92 – Snake.
34. #94 – Pig.
35. #98 – Dragon.
36. #102 – Mermaid.
37. #104 – Wild Cat.
38. #107 – Fox.
39. #111 – Hummingbird.
40. #112 – Cat.
41. #116 – Fish.
42. #118 – Deer.
43. #121 – Raccoon.
44. #123 – Daisy.
45. #126 – Basil.
46. #128 – Rose.
47. #135 – Tulip.
48. #136 – Sakura.
49. #139 – Bamboo.
50. #142 – Lily.
51. #145 – Violet.
52. #146 – Tomato.
53. #148 – Yucca.
54. #152 – Calathea.
55. #156 – USB Drive.
56. #158 – Computer.
57. #160 – Assembly Line.
58. #162 – Air Conditioner.
59. #164 – Plane.

60. #166 – Headphones.
61. #171 – Internet.
62. #175 – Remote.
63. #179 – Stove/Oven.
64. #182 – Surgical Implant.
65. #185 – Enraged.
66. #188 – Joyful.
67. #190 – Fearful.
68. #192 – Sad.
69. #195 – Boredom.
70. #198 – Sleepy.
71. #200 – Resentful.
72. #203 – Jealous.
73. #205 – Annoyed.
74. #208 – Curious.
75. #211 – Disgusted.
76. #214 – Awkward.
77. #217 – Wizard.
78. #220 – Brewing Pot.
79. #223 – Potion Ingredients.
80. #226 – Wand.
81. #228 – Water Witch/Wizard.
82. #231 – Air Witch/Wizard.
83. #237 – Broom Stick.
84. #239 – Magical Boy.
85. #243 – Scroll Shop.
86. #246 – Jeans.
87. #248 – Shorts.
88. #251 – Leather Jacket.
89. #254 – Graphic Tee.
90. #258 – Onesie.
91. #261 – Stockings.
92. #264 – Vest.
93. #267 – Scarf.
94. #270 – Hoodie.
95. #273 – Boots.
96. #275 – Nude.
97. #278 – Nap Time.
98. #280 – Movies.
99. #283 – Take A Walk.

Acrylic Paint (AP)

8. #18 – Spy/Secret Agent.
9. #22 – Scientist.
10. #27 – Athlete.
11. #30 – Dungeon.
12. #33 – Dry.
13. #35 – Soft.
14. #37 – Rough.
15. #40 – Slick.
16. #42 – Toned.
17. #44 – Smooth.
18. #47 – Gooey.
19. #49 – Rubbery.
20. #51 – Feathery.
21. #53 – Cotton.
22. #57 – Glass.
23. #59 – Silicone.
24. #61 – Sitting.
25. #64 – Stretching.
26. #65 – Pin-up.
27. #68 – Salsa Dancing.
28. #70 – Jumping Jacks.
29. #72 – Spinning.
30. #75 – Kissing.
31. #78 – Laying.
32. #81 – Punching.
33. #83 – Tiptoeing.
34. #85 – Hiding.
35. #89 – Hugging.
36. #92 – Snake.
37. #95 – Rabbit.
38. #97 – Chicken.
39. #99 – Frog.
40. #100 – Sheep.
41. #103 – Whale.
42. #105 – Elephant.
43. #106 – Polar Bear.
44. #109 – Phoenix.
45. #110 – Crab.
46. #113 – Dolphin.
47. #115 – Reptile.

48. #118 – Deer.
49. #120 – Chipmunk.
50. #122 – Sunflower.
51. #125 – Cactus.
52. #127 – Jasmine.
53. #129 – Mint.
54. #131 – Spinach.
55. #133 – Snake Plant.
56. #135 – Tulip.
57. #136 – Sakura.
58. #138 – Aloe Vera.
59. #141 – Lily Pad.
60. #143 – Fern.
61. #144 – Lilac.
62. #146 – Tomato.
63. #149 – Spider Plant.
64. #152 – Calathea.
65. #155 – CD.
66. #157 – Television.
67. #159 – Car.
68. #161 – iPod.
69. #163 – Hair Dryer.
70. #165 – Camera.
71. #167 – Robot.
72. #169 – VR Headset.
73. #171 – Internet.
74. #174 – Vending Machine.
75. #177 – Speaker.
76. #180 – Refrigerator.
77. #184 – Awed.
78. #187 – Desperate.
79. #189 – Excited.
80. #192 – Sad.
81. #194 – Love.
82. #197 – Depressed.
83. #199 – Hopeful.
84. #201 – Guilty.
85. #204 – Lonely.
86. #206 – Stressed.
87. #209 – Cautious.

88. #213 – Nostalgic.
89. #216 – Spell.
90. #218 – Witch.
91. #220 – Brewing Pot.
92. #222 – Magic Trick.
93. #224 – Scroll.
94. #226 – Wand.
95. #230 – Earth Witch/Wizard.
96. #232 – Necromancer.
97. #235 – Spell Book.
98. #237 – Broom Stick.
99. #240 – Bottomless Bag.
100. #242 – Potion Shop.
101. #245 – Cardigan.
102. #247 – T-Shirt.
103. #250 – Romper.
104. #253 – Beanie.
105. #256 – Dress.
106. #260 – Blouse.
107. #262 – Jumpsuit.
108. #264 – Vest.
109. #266 – Sandals.
110. #269 – Crop Top.
111. #272 – Leggings.
112. #274 – Sweater.
113. #276 – Bubble Bath.
114. #279 – Cuddles.
115. #282 – Painting Nails.
116. #285 – Hang out with a friend.
117. #288 – Favorite Meal.
118. #291 – Mantra.
119. #294 – Family Time.
120. #296 – New Place.
121. #300 – Treat Yourself.
122. #302 – Unplug.
123. #305 – Hair.
124. #308 – Burgundy.
125. #310 – Pine Green.
126. #313 – Violet.
127. #316 – Mustard.

128. #319 – White.
129. #322 – Purple.
130. #325 – Lilac Purple.
131. #327 – Ivory.
132. #330 – Sea-Foam Green.
133. #332 – Navy Blue.
134. #335 – Bronze.
135. #337 – Dessert.
136. #339 – Milkshake.
137. #342 – Sandwich.
138. #345 – Coffee.
139. #348 – Ice-cream.
140. #351 – Carrots.
141. #354 – Bubble Tea.
142. #356 – Muffin.
143. #358 – Lemonade.
144. #360 – Mac & Cheese.
145. #362 – Steak.
146. #364 – Hot Chocolate.

Watercolor (W)

1. #1 – Ballerina.
2. #4 – Doctor.
3. #6 – Mentor.
4. #7 – Tiny House.
5. #10 – Child.
6. #12 – Hero/Heroine.
7. #16 – Concert.
8. #19 – Model.
9. #22 – Scientist.
10. #23 – House.
11. #25 – Circus.
12. #28 – Alien.
13. #30 – Dungeon.
14. #31 – Bookstore.
15. #34 – Wrinkled.
16. #37 – Rough.
17. #39 – Chiseled.

18. #41 – Greasy.
19. #43 – Cracked.
20. #46 – Hairy.
21. #49 – Rubbery.
22. #51 – Feathery.
23. #56 – Wooden.
24. #59 – Silicone.
25. #60 – Canvas.
26. #63 – Jumping.
27. #66 – Crawling.
28. #69 – Sliding.
29. #71 – Running.
30. #73 – Sneaking.
31. #76 – Rolling.
32. #77 – Playing.
33. #80 – Crouching.
34. #82 – Kicking.
35. #84 – Licking.
36. #85 – Hiding.
37. #89 – Hugging.
38. #91 – Waving.
39. #94 – Pig.
40. #96 – Dog.
41. #98 – Dragon.
42. #100 – Sheep.
43. #102 – Mermaid.
44. #104 – Wild Cat.
45. #107 – Fox.
46. #109 – Phoenix.
47. #111 – Hummingbird.
48. #112 – Cat.
49. #114 – Monkey.
50. #117 – Goat.
51. #121 – Raccoon.
52. #123 – Daisy.
53. #125 – Cactus.
54. #129 – Mint.
55. #132 – Rubber Plant.
56. #138 – Aloe Vera.
57. #140 – Peony.

58. #143 – Fern.
59. #145 – Violet.
60. #147 – Green Onion.
61. #149 – Spider Plant.
62. #151 – Venus Fly Trap.
63. #153 – Phone.
64. #154 – Radio.
65. #156 – USB Drive.
66. #159 – Car.
67. #163 – Hair Dryer.
68. #167 – Robot.
69. #169 – VR Headset.
70. #173 – X-Ray Machine.
71. #175 – Remote.
72. #178 – Tracker.
73. #181 – Credit/Debit Card.
74. #183 – Robotic Limb.
75. #187 – Desperate.
76. #190 – Fearful.
77. #192 – Sad.
78. #196 – Anticipation.
79. #199 – Hopeful.
80. #200 – Resentful.
81. #202 – Invincible.
82. #205 – Annoyed.
83. #208 – Curious.
84. #210 – Skeptical.
85. #213 – Nostalgic.
86. #215 – Potion.
87. #218 – Witch.
88. #221 – Magician.
89. #223 – Potion Ingredients.
90. #226 – Wand.
91. #229 – Fire Witch/Wizard.
92. #232 – Necromancer.
93. #234 – Magic Creature.
94. #236 – Disappearing.
95. #238 – Magical Girl.
96. #239 – Magical Boy.
97. #241 – Witch/Wizard's Home.

98. #244 – Magical Professor.
99. #247 – T-Shirt.
100. #249 – Pajamas.
101. #251 – Leather Jacket.
102. #253 – Beanie.
103. #255 – Robe.
104. #257 – Swimsuit.
105. #259 – Pencil Skirt.
106. #262 – Jumpsuit.
107. #265 – Sneakers.
108. #267 – Scarf.
109. #270 – Hoodie.
110. #273 – Boots.
111. #276 – Bubble Bath.
112. #280 – Movies.
113. #283 – Take A Walk.
114. #285 – Hang out with a friend.
115. #287 – Exercise.
116. #289 – Diary Entry.
117. #291 – Mantra.
118. #293 – Nostalgia.
119. #296 – New Place.
120. #299 – Favorite Music.
121. #302 – Unplug.
122. #305 – Hair.
123. #307 – Yellow.
124. #310 – Pine Green.
125. #313 – Violet.
126. #315 – Red-Orange.
127. #317 – Brown.
128. #320 – Black.
129. #322 – Purple.
130. #324 – Mint Green.
131. #328 – Hazel.
132. #331 – Peach.
133. #335 – Bronze.
134. #337 – Dessert.
135. #339 – Milkshake.
136. #343 – Banana Pancakes.
137. #345 – Coffee.

138. #347 – Bacon, Egg, & Cheese.
139. #350 – Cake.
140. #353 – Sushi.
141. #356 – Muffin.
142. #358 – Lemonade.
143. #361 – Eggs.
144. #365 – Ramen.

Ink (I)

1. #2 – Police Station.
2. #5 – Meadow.
3. #7 – Tiny House.
4. #9 – Fort.
5. #12 – Hero/Heroine.
6. #13 – Witch.
7. #15 – City.
8. #18 – Spy/Secret Agent.
9. #20 – Space.
10. #22 – Scientist.
11. #23 – House.
12. #25 – Circus.
13. #28 – Alien.
14. #29 – Amusement Park.
15. #33 – Dry.
16. #35 – Soft.
17. #36 – Shiny.
18. #39 – Chiseled.
19. #41 – Greasy.
20. #43 – Cracked.
21. #45 – Scratchy.
22. #47 – Gooey.
23. #49 – Rubbery.
24. #52 – Jean.
25. #57 – Glass.
26. #60 – Canvas.
27. #62 – Sleeping.
28. #63 – Jumping.
29. #66 – Crawling.

30. #67 – Break Dancing.
31. #70 – Jumping Jacks.
32. #71 – Running.
33. #74 – Walking.
34. #77 – Playing.
35. #80 – Crouching.
36. #84 – Licking.
37. #86 – Blocking.
38. #88 – Praying.
39. #90 – Pointing.
40. #91 – Waving.
41. #93 – Turtle.
42. #95 – Rabbit.
43. #97 – Chicken.
44. #99 – Frog.
45. #101 – Wolf.
46. #103 – Whale.
47. #105 – Elephant.
48. #108 – Extinct Animal.
49. #113 – Dolphin.
50. #115 – Reptile.
51. #118 – Deer.
52. #122 – Sunflower.
53. #125 – Cactus.
54. #126 – Basil.
55. #129 – Mint.
56. #131 – Spinach.
57. #133 – Snake Plant.
58. #134 – Orchid.
59. #136 – Sakura.
60. #140 – Peony.
61. #142 – Lily.
62. #146 – Tomato.
63. #149 – Spider Plant.
64. #151 – Venus Fly Trap.
65. #153 – Phone.
66. #155 – CD.
67. #158 – Computer.
68. #160 – Assembly Line.
69. #162 – Air Conditioner.

70. #164 – Plane.
71. #165 – Camera.
72. #168 – Console Game.
73. #170 – Train.
74. #172 – Hearing Aid.
75. #173 – X-Ray Machine.
76. #177 – Speaker.
77. #179 – Stove/Oven.
78. #181 – Credit/Debit Card.
79. #184 – Awed.
80. #186 – Confused.
81. #188 – Joyful.
82. #190 – Fearful.
83. #193 – Hyper.
84. #194 – Love.
85. #196 – Anticipation.
86. #198 – Sleepy.
87. #202 – Invincible.
88. #205 – Annoyed.
89. #207 – Protective.
90. #210 – Skeptical.
91. #214 – Awkward.
92. #217 – Wizard.
93. #219 – Curse.
94. #221 – Magician.
95. #224 – Scroll.
96. #227 – Witch's Hat.
97. #229 – Fire Witch/Wizard.
98. #231 – Air Witch/Wizard.
99. #233 – Sorcerer.
100. #236 – Disappearing.
101. #238 – Magical Girl.
102. #240 – Bottomless Bag.
103. #241 – Witch/Wizard's Home.
104. #245 – Cardigan.
105. #248 – Shorts.
106. #249 – Pajamas.
107. #252 – Fitted Cap.
108. #255 – Robe.
109. #258 – Onesie.

110. #260 – Blouse.
111. #263 – Winter Coat.
112. #267 – Scarf.
113. #269 – Crop Top.
114. #271 – Fedora.
115. #274 – Sweater.
116. #276 – Bubble Bath.
117. #278 – Nap Time.
118. #281 – Meditation.
119. #282 – Painting Nails.
120. #284 – Declutter.
121. #286 – Massage.
122. #289 – Diary Entry.
123. #291 – Mantra.
124. #293 – Nostalgia.
125. #296 – New Place.
126. #298 – Doodle.
127. #301 – Gratitude List.
128. #303 – Coloring Book.
129. #305 – Hair.
130. #307 – Yellow.
131. #309 – Lime Green.
132. #312 – Orange.
133. #315 – Red-Orange.
134. #317 – Brown.
135. #319 – White.
136. #321 – Sky Blue.
137. #323 – Red.
138. #325 – Lilac Purple.
139. #327 – Ivory.
140. #330 – Sea-Foam Green.
141. #333 – Taupe.
142. #336 – Rainbow.
143. #337 – Dessert.
144. #341 – Spaghetti.
145. #344 – Taco.
146. #346 – Water.
147. #348 – Ice-cream.
148. #350 – Cake.
149. #353 – Sushi.

150. #355 – Chips.
151. #359 – Salad.
152. #361 – Eggs.
153. #364 – Hot Chocolate.

Gouache (G)

1. #2 – Police Station.
2. #4 – Doctor.
3. #6 – Mentor.
4. #9 – Fort.
5. #11 – Beach.
6. #14 – Temple.
7. #15 – City.
8. #18 – Spy/Secret Agent.
9. #21 – Tropical Island.
10. #24 – Inventor.
11. #26 – Artist.
12. #29 – Amusement Park.
13. #31 – Bookstore.
14. #32 – Slimy.
15. #36 – Shiny.
16. #38 – Fuzzy.
17. #41 – Greasy.
18. #44 – Smooth.
19. #48 – Leathery.
20. #50 – Metallic.
21. #52 – Jean.
22. #54 – Stretchy.
23. #58 – Plastic.
24. #62 – Sleeping.
25. #64 – Stretching.
26. #67 – Break Dancing.
27. #69 – Sliding.
28. #72 – Spinning.
29. #74 – Walking.
30. #75 – Kissing.
31. #78 – Laying.
32. #80 – Crouching.

33. #81 – Punching.
34. #84 – Licking.
35. #86 – Blocking.
36. #87 – Fighting.
37. #89 – Hugging.
38. #92 – Snake.
39. #95 – Rabbit.
40. #96 – Dog.
41. #99 – Frog.
42. #101 – Wolf.
43. #102 – Mermaid.
44. #106 – Polar Bear.
45. #108 – Extinct Animal.
46. #110 – Crab.
47. #113 – Dolphin.
48. #115 – Reptile.
49. #117 – Goat.
50. #119 – Shark.
51. #120 – Chipmunk.
52. #123 – Daisy.
53. #124 – Pumpkin.
54. #127 – Jasmine.
55. #128 – Rose.
56. #131 – Spinach.
57. #132 – Rubber Plant.
58. #134 – Orchid.
59. #137 – Lavender.
60. #139 – Bamboo.
61. #142 – Lily.
62. #145 – Violet.
63. #148 – Yucca.
64. #150 – Philodendron.
65. #154 – Radio.
66. #155 – CD.
67. #157 – Television.
68. #162 – Air Conditioner.
69. #166 – Headphones.
70. #168 – Console Game.
71. #171 – Internet.
72. #174 – Vending Machine.

73. #176 – GPS.
74. #178 – Tracker.
75. #180 – Refrigerator.
76. #182 – Surgical Implant.
77. #185 – Enraged.
78. #189 – Excited.
79. #193 – Hyper.
80. #195 – Boredom.
81. #197 – Depressed.
82. #200 – Resentful.
83. #203 – Jealous.
84. #207 – Protective.
85. #209 – Cautious.
86. #211 – Disgusted.
87. #212 – Judgmental.
88. #216 – Spell.
89. #219 – Curse.
90. #222 – Magic Trick.
91. #225 – Magic School.
92. #228 – Water Witch/Wizard.
93. #230 – Earth Witch/Wizard.
94. #232 – Necromancer.
95. #234 – Magic Creature.
96. #235 – Spell Book.
97. #238 – Magical Girl.
98. #240 – Bottomless Bag.
99. #242 – Potion Shop.
100. #244 – Magical Professor.
101. #246 – Jeans.
102. #248 – Shorts.
103. #250 – Romper.
104. #252 – Fitted Cap.
105. #253 – Beanie.
106. #256 – Dress.
107. #258 – Onesie.
108. #260 – Blouse.
109. #263 – Winter Coat.
110. #265 – Sneakers.
111. #268 – Button-up.
112. #271 – Fedora.

113. #274 – Sweater.
114. #277 – Face Mask.
115. #279 – Cuddles.
116. #281 – Meditation.
117. #284 – Declutter.
118. #286 – Massage.
119. #288 – Favorite Meal.
120. #292 – Bird Watching.
121. #295 – Cloud Watching.
122. #298 – Doodle.
123. #300 – Treat Yourself.
124. #303 – Coloring Book.
125. #306 – Teal.
126. #312 – Orange.
127. #315 – Red-Orange.
128. #318 – Pastel.
129. #320 – Black.
130. #323 – Red.
131. #325 – Lilac Purple.
132. #328 – Hazel.
133. #330 – Sea-Foam Green.
134. #333 – Taupe.
135. #335 – Bronze.
136. #338 – Pizza.
137. #340 – Tea.
138. #342 – Sandwich.
139. #344 – Taco.
140. #347 – Bacon, Egg, & Cheese.
141. #349 – French Fries.
142. #352 – Fried Rice.
143. #354 – Bubble Tea.
144. #357 – Candy.
145. #360 – Mac & Cheese.
146. #363 – Vegan.

Marker (M)

1. #1 – Ballerina.
2. #3 – Mountain.

3. #8 – Parents.
4. #11 – Beach.
5. #13 – Witch.
6. #15 – City.
7. #17 – Band.
8. #19 – Model.
9. #21 – Tropical Island.
10. #24 – Inventor.
11. #26 – Artist.
12. #28 – Alien.
13. #32 – Slimy.
14. #34 – Wrinkled.
15. #39 – Chiseled.
16. #42 – Toned.
17. #45 – Scratchy.
18. #46 – Hairy.
19. #48 – Leathery.
20. #50 – Metallic.
21. #53 – Cotton.
22. #57 – Glass.
23. #61 – Sitting.
24. #64 – Stretching.
25. #66 – Crawling.
26. #68 – Salsa Dancing.
27. #70 – Jumping Jacks.
28. #72 – Spinning.
29. #74 – Walking.
30. #76 – Rolling.
31. #79 – Standing.
32. #82 – Kicking.
33. #85 – Hiding.
34. #87 – Fighting.
35. #90 – Pointing.
36. #94 – Pig.
37. #96 – Dog.
38. #98 – Dragon.
39. #100 – Sheep.
40. #104 – Wild Cat.
41. #106 – Polar Bear.
42. #108 – Extinct Animal.

43. #112 – Cat.
44. #116 – Fish.
45. #119 – Shark.
46. #121 – Raccoon.
47. #122 – Sunflower.
48. #126 – Basil.
49. #128 – Rose.
50. #130 – Vines.
51. #133 – Snake Plant.
52. #135 – Tulip.
53. #137 – Lavender.
54. #139 – Bamboo.
55. #141 – Lily Pad.
56. #144 – Lilac.
57. #148 – Yucca.
58. #151 – Venus Fly Trap.
59. #153 – Phone.
60. #154 – Radio.
61. #156 – USB Drive.
62. #158 – Computer.
63. #161 – iPod.
64. #164 – Plane.
65. #167 – Robot.
66. #170 – Train.
67. #172 – Hearing Aid.
68. #174 – Vending Machine.
69. #176 – GPS.
70. #179 – Stove/Oven.
71. #182 – Surgical Implant.
72. #183 – Robotic Limb.
73. #186 – Confused.
74. #187 – Desperate.
75. #189 – Excited.
76. #191 – Anxious.
77. #194 – Love.
78. #197 – Depressed.
79. #199 – Hopeful.
80. #201 – Guilty.
81. #203 – Jealous.
82. #206 – Stressed.

83. #209 – Cautious.
84. #212 – Judgmental.
85. #214 – Awkward.
86. #216 – Spell.
87. #218 – Witch.
88. #219 – Curse.
89. #222 – Magic Trick.
90. #224 – Scroll.
91. #227 – Witch's Hat.
92. #229 – Fire Witch/Wizard.
93. #233 – Sorcerer.
94. #236 – Disappearing.
95. #242 – Potion Shop.
96. #244 – Magical Professor.
97. #246 – Jeans.
98. #249 – Pajamas.
99. #252 – Fitted Cap.
100. #255 – Robe.
101. #257 – Swimsuit.
102. #261 – Stockings.
103. #263 – Winter Coat.
104. #266 – Sandals.
105. #268 – Button-up.
106. #270 – Hoodie.
107. #272 – Leggings.
108. #275 – Nude.
109. #278 – Nap Time.
110. #281 – Meditation.
111. #284 – Declutter.
112. #287 – Exercise.
113. #290 – Create.
114. #293 – Nostalgia.
115. #295 – Cloud Watching.
116. #297 – Favorite Activity.
117. #300 – Treat Yourself.
118. #304 – Favorite Dessert.
119. #308 – Burgundy.
120. #310 – Pine Green.
121. #312 – Orange.
122. #314 – Pink.

123. #316 – Mustard.
124. #318 – Pastel.
125. #322 – Purple.
126. #326 – Silver.
127. #329 – Mocha.
128. #331 – Peach.
129. #334 – Gold.
130. #338 – Pizza.
131. #340 – Tea.
132. #342 – Sandwich.
133. #344 – Taco.
134. #346 – Water.
135. #348 – Ice-cream.
136. #351 – Carrots.
137. #353 – Sushi.
138. #356 – Muffin.
139. #359 – Salad.
140. #363 – Vegan.

Crayon (C)

1. #3 – Mountain.
2. #5 – Meadow.
3. #8 – Parents.
4. #9 – Fort.
5. #14 – Temple.
6. #16 – Concert.
7. #20 – Space.
8. #24 – Inventor.
9. #29 – Amusement Park.
10. #36 – Shiny.
11. #42 – Toned.
12. #44 – Smooth.
13. #48 – Leathery.
14. #51 – Feathery.
15. #53 – Cotton.
16. #56 – Wooden.
17. #58 – Plastic.
18. #61 – Sitting.

19. #65 – Pin-up.
20. #68 – Salsa Dancing.
21. #71 – Running.
22. #78 – Laying.
23. #81 – Punching.
24. #88 – Praying.
25. #90 – Pointing.
26. #93 – Turtle.
27. #105 – Elephant.
28. #107 – Fox.
29. #110 – Crab.
30. #114 – Monkey.
31. #116 – Fish.
32. #119 – Shark.
33. #124 – Pumpkin.
34. #130 – Vines.
35. #134 – Orchid.
36. #137 – Lavender.
37. #140 – Peony.
38. #144 – Lilac.
39. #147 – Green Onion.
40. #150 – Philodendron.
41. #152 – Calathea.
42. #160 – Assembly Line.
43. #165 – Camera.
44. #169 – VR Headset.
45. #173 – X-Ray Machine.
46. #177 – Speaker.
47. #181 – Credit/Debit Card.
48. #184 – Awed.
49. #186 – Confused.
50. #191 – Anxious.
51. #196 – Anticipation.
52. #202 – Invincible.
53. #204 – Lonely.
54. #207 – Protective.
55. #211 – Disgusted.
56. #212 – Judgmental.
57. #215 – Potion.
58. #221 – Magician.

59. #225 – Magic School.
60. #228 – Water Witch/Wizard.
61. #231 – Air Witch/Wizard.
62. #234 – Magic Creature.
63. #237 – Broom Stick.
64. #243 – Scroll Shop.
65. #247 – T-Shirt.
66. #251 – Leather Jacket.
67. #254 – Graphic Tee.
68. #257 – Swimsuit.
69. #259 – Pencil Skirt.
70. #261 – Stockings.
71. #265 – Sneakers.
72. #269 – Crop Top.
73. #272 – Leggings.
74. #275 – Nude.
75. #277 – Face Mask.
76. #279 – Cuddles.
77. #282 – Painting Nails.
78. #286 – Massage.
79. #290 – Create.
80. #294 – Family Time.
81. #297 – Favorite Activity.
82. #299 – Favorite Music.
83. #301 – Gratitude List.
84. #304 – Favorite Dessert.
85. #307 – Yellow.
86. #309 – Lime Green.
87. #311 – Royal Blue.
88. #314 – Pink.
89. #317 – Brown.
90. #320 – Black.
91. #323 – Red.
92. #326 – Silver.
93. #329 – Mocha.
94. #332 – Navy Blue.
95. #334 – Gold.
96. #338 – Pizza.
97. #341 – Spaghetti.
98. #345 – Coffee.

99. #349 – French Fries.
100. #352 – Fried Rice.
101. #354 – Bubble Tea.
102. #357 – Candy.
103. #359 – Salad.
104. #362 – Steak.
105. #365 – Ramen.

Drawing Exercises

1. Go out and sketch your favorite place to hang out.
2. Draw a realistic portrait of your best friend.
3. Draw the exterior of your dream home.
4. Draw what your house looks like during your favorite holiday.
5. Draw yourself as a fantasy creature (i.e. elf, orc, etc.)
6. Draw yourself in your ideal career.
7. Draw 10 items that are shiny.
8. Draw 10 things that are rigid.
9. Draw 10 things that are soft.
10. Draw 10 things that are stretchy.
11. Draw 10 things that are smooth.
12. Draw 10 things that are fuzzy.
13. Draw someone posing for a professional photoshoot.
14. Draw someone's reaction to being scared.
15. Draw a dog ready to play.
16. Draw someone who is ready to fight.
17. Draw someone pretending to be surprised.
18. Draw someone posing to admire their muscles.
19. Draw 5 different types of birds.
20. Draw 5 different animals sleeping.
21. Draw 5 different types of dogs.
22. Draw 5 different animals attacking.
23. Draw 5 different types of cats.
24. Draw 5 different animals playing.
25. Draw a plant during three different stages of growth.
26. Draw a plant that is wilting.
27. Draw a garden of your favorite fruit/vegetables.
28. Draw a bouquet of your favorite flowers.
29. Draw an animal grazing on some plants.
30. Draw your ideal salad.
31. Draw 5 different types of phones.
32. Draw 5 different types of game consoles/controllers.
33. Draw 5 different types of cameras.
34. Draw 5 different methods of transportation.
35. Draw 5 different types of cooking tools (i.e. blender, oven, microwave, etc.).

36. Draw 5 different types of computers.
37. Draw 5 different expressions of joy.
38. Draw 5 different expressions of sorrow.
39. Draw 5 different expressions of love.
40. Draw 5 different expressions of anger.
41. Draw 5 different expressions of anxiety.
42. Draw 5 different expressions of surprise.
43. Draw a collection of scrolls.
44. Draw a collection of potions.
45. Draw a collection of magic broom sticks.
46. Draw a collection of magic wands.
47. Draw a collection of witch/wizard hats.
48. Draw a group of magical creatures.
49. Draw an outfit with a goth aesthetic.
50. Draw an outfit with a retro aesthetic.
51. Draw an outfit with a witchy aesthetic.
52. Draw an outfit with a professional aesthetic.
53. Draw an outfit with an athletic aesthetic.
54. Draw an outfit with a hipster aesthetic.
55. Draw an outfit with a nerdy aesthetic.
56. Draw 5 items involved in a spa day.
57. Draw 5 items involved with taking a nap.
58. Draw 5 items involved with preparing your favorite meal.
59. Draw 5 items involved with having a movie night.
60. Draw 5 items involved with playing games.
61. Draw 5 items involved with doing your hair.
62. Draw 10 things that are primarily red.
63. Draw 10 things that are primarily blue.
64. Draw 10 things that are primarily yellow.
65. Draw 10 things that are primarily black.
66. Draw 10 things that are primarily green.
67. Draw 10 things that are primarily white.
68. Draw a plate of your favorite fruits.
69. Draw a plate of your favorite vegetables.
70. Draw 5 desserts that you like.
71. Draw 5 breakfast items that you like.
72. Draw 5 beverages that you like.
73. Draw 5 snacks that you like.

Thank You!

That's all for now! We hope you had fun exploring your creative side! If you did, please considering leaving us a review. We'd really appreciate it!

You can come back next year for our 2021 edition and do a whole new set of prompts, and a new set of exercises.

But in the meantime, if you're looking for something to keep you busy, you can try our other prompt books:

- 365 Writing Prompts.
- 100 Character Prompts.
- 100 Quote Prompts.
- And more!

And if you're looking for something fun to read to give you some inspiration, check out our fiction books and comics!

For more information, check out our website, www.TCStudiosHQ.com.